D1307406

WHO ARE THESE SALVATIONISTS?
An Analysis for the 21st Century

Also by Shaw Clifton:

What Does the Salvationist Say? (London: Salvationist Publishing and Supplies, 1977).

Growing Together (London: The Salvation Army, 1984). With Helen Clifton.

Strong Doctrine, Strong Mercy (London: The Salvation Army, 1985).

Never the Same Again (Alexandria, VA: Crest Books, 1997).

WHO ARE THESE SALVATIONISTS?
An Analysis for the 21st Century

Shaw Clifton

Crest Books
Salvation Army National Publications
615 Slaters Lane
Alexandria, VA 22313

copyright ©1999 Salvation Army National Publications

Published by Crest Books, Salvation Army National Publications
615 Slaters Lane
Alexandria, VA 22313
Phone: (703) 684-5500
Fax: (703) 684-5539
http://publications.salvationarmyusa.org

Printed in the United States of America.

All rights reserved. No part of this publication may be reproduced, stored in a retrieval system or transmitted in any form or by any means—electronic, mechanical, photocopy, recording—without the prior written permission of the publisher. The only exception is brief quotes in printed reviews.

Unless otherwise noted, Scripture taken from the *Holy Bible, New International Version*. Copyright ©1973, 1978, 1984 by the International Bible Society. Used by permission. All rights reserved.

Library of Congress Catalog Card Number: 99–61285

ISBN: 0–9657601–6–2

For Helen

Contents

Preface

In May of 1997, it was my privilege to be the Chandler Memorial Lecturer at The Salvation Army School for Officer Training in the Eastern territory of the United States. These annual lectures honor the life of Colonel Alfred Augustus Chandler, an Englishman who served as an officer of The Salvation Army not only in his homeland, but also in the United States of America (1898 to 1910, and 1920 to retirement in 1930) and Canada (1910 to 1920). He was highly influential in shaping the officer training programs of the Army in America. At the inception of the Southern territory of the United States in 1926, Chandler was appointed its first chief secretary. He was later appointed as chief secretary of the Eastern territory in the United States.

The Chandler Memorial Lectures are open to the public and are intended to address issues in contemporary Christian mission from theological, biblical, historical and social science perspectives, as a stimulus to reflective action for the salvation of the world.

The four sections of this book are extended versions of four lectures delivered in 1997. It is my hope and prayer that the material, which here and there has deliberately been allowed to retain its college lecture origins, will stimulate Salvationist readers to further reflection upon our identity as an Army of God and as part of the body of Christ on earth, and that our many and valued non-Salvationist friends will find much in these pages to deepen their understanding of the Army as we enter the twenty–first century.

Each of the four parts can be read as separate units, but later sections sometimes assume the preceding sections have been perused first. The prologues differ in style and content from the main chapters, offering background and atmosphere for what follows. Readers in a hurry might decide to pass over the sustained illustrations in the special case studies in chapters 8 and 12, but in so doing will miss much that underscores in grassroots experience the principles under analysis.

In using the four themes of Protestant evangelicalism, sacramentalism, pragmatism and internationalism, I do not intend to suggest that these are the only bases on which Salvation Army distinctives can be discussed. They do, however, provide a contemporary opportunity to explore who we were, who we are, and who we ought to be in the twenty–first century.

S. C.

Author's Acknowledgments

This material was first compiled in Boston, Massachusetts early in 1997. The book manuscript was finalized in Lahore, Pakistan in the Fall of 1998. I express warmest thanks to Lt. Colonel Marlene Chase, USA National Editor in Chief and Literary Secretary, for her vision, unfailing encouragement and patience. I am indebted also to the splendid team that works under her leadership, and to those who examined the manuscript in first draft and offered penetrating but kindly comment.

Part I
Salvationists as Protestant Evangelicals

Prologue
Encounter with a Cardinal

Boston, Massachusetts is a great city and New England a beautiful part of America. However, the time had come to leave. Two short years had passed since arriving from the United Kingdom to take charge of the Salvation Army's Massachusetts division, and now my wife and I were under instructions to pack up again. This time we were heading for Pakistan!

One of the joys of being in Massachusetts had been the enriching contacts with other church leaders, mostly through the Massachusetts Council of Churches, but also with Roman Catholic leaders who were not formally part of the Council. Boston is a Catholic stronghold; of all those attending church on Sundays, half are Roman Catholics. The Cardinal Archbishop of Boston is an immensely influential figure in the life of the city. So it was that on a sunny June morning in 1997 I found myself heading for the official residence of Cardinal Bernard Law in Brighton, a pleasant, leafy Boston suburb. Hearing of my impending departure for pastures new, he had asked me to drop by for coffee and a chat.

"Would you like orange juice with your coffee and Danish?" Cardinal Law's familiar, resonant tones boomed from the corridor.

A moment later he swept into the room with a tray bearing coffee pot, cups and pastries, to be closely followed by the diminutive figure of a nun dressed all in white and murmuring, "Oh dear, the Cardinal is serving you himself!"

From the first time I had met him over a working breakfast two years earlier, I had taken a liking to this man. Even though we hailed from vastly different traditions, I came to know him as a highly intelligent, friendly and unashamedly Roman Catholic advocate for the gospel. Furthermore, we found ourselves not far apart when it came to the pressing ethical issues of the day.

That morning the small talk ended quickly, and we got down to substantive things—the state of Christianity in Pakistan, the situation of the Roman Catholic church there, the problems of evangelizing in a Moslem culture, the Cardinal's willingness to write letters of introduction for me to the Catholic prelates there. Then the surprise! Suddenly the Cardinal was reflecting aloud about the relationship between The Salvation Army and the Church of Rome! What was this? Was I hearing him correctly?

"Of all the Protestant groups today, it is The Salvation Army that represents the best chance of entering into full communion with Rome," he said. I glanced across at my friend and colleague, now Lt. Colonel Gilbert Reynders, who was to succeed me and who would need to relate closely to church leaders like the Cardinal. Had he grasped the enormous significance of what had just been said? "I'm serious," continued the Cardinal, "for I see The Salvation Army as an authentic expression of classical Christianity. You are clear about the person and nature of Jesus Christ. You are close to Rome on many ethical issues. You have stood shoulder to shoulder with us here in Boston to confront the culture of death and abortion. The ordination of your officers is for function and good order within the denomination and would not be an issue affecting priesthood."

I looked at him intently. Clearly, he meant it. It was a new experience for me. Here I was, sitting in the Cardinal's boardroom at the end of the table where an inscription recorded that Pope John Paul II had sat there also, and I was listening to a prince of the Church of Rome outline his vision for Rome absorbing The Salvation

Army! We went on to discuss our roots in Wesleyan Methodism, our stance on women in ministry and the nature of Salvationist sacramentalism with its absence of sacramental ritual.

"My ideas may sound pretty weird I suppose," he concluded.

"Not so," was my rejoinder, "even if you are the only person in the world who thinks this way! Any suggestion that comes from a loving heart and is born of a desire to see God's people more visibly united deserves both an airing and a considered response."

He showed us his private chapel, wished me well for the future, and with warm handshakes all round we took our leave.

"An authentic expression of classical Christianity." It was one of the most perceptive things I had ever heard said about the Army.

Chapter 1
Is The Salvation Army a Church?

Historical Development • A Church? • The Theological
Approach • The Sociological Approach • The Legal Approach

Is The Salvation Army a church? I know what the answer would
have been had I put this question bluntly to Cardinal Law. Despite
his obvious warmth and respectful goodwill, he would have smiled
and said gently, "The Army is not a church, but an order."

This is a view often expressed, and not only by those within
the Roman Catholic church. Anyone having what is known as a
"high" ecclesiology will draw the same conclusion, for their initial
definition and theological understanding of what constitutes a
church includes the practice of some form of the traditional
sacraments as an essential characteristic of an authentic church. I
recently met an Anglo–Asian gentleman here in Lahore who had
started attending our Sunday morning worship service. He fell into
conversation with one of my missionary colleagues and explained
that he belonged to the Church of Pakistan (an amalgam of
Anglicans, Lutherans, Methodists and Presbyterians). He went on
to comment that he could not regard the Army as a true church
because his priest had informed him that the Army had no
sacraments and could not therefore be seen as a church. My
colleague's response was a model of holy restraint!

Those who have a broader grasp of "church" and whose eccle-siology is "low," for instance those from evangelical, free church, and Protestant backgrounds, are much more open to the idea that the Army is a church, a distinctive Christian denomination. They understand the fallacy of describing the Army as an order, for they see the Army's independence from any other denominational structure. Those who tell us we are merely an order do not go on to any logical conclusion; they do not think it through.

Traditionally, an order in the church is a subdivision or part of a larger ecclesiastical body. The Jesuits, for example, are an order within the Church of Rome. The Church Army is an order of evangelists within the Church of England (having been instituted as a direct Anglican response to the rise of The Salvation Army and the eventual failure of overtures made by the Church of England to William Booth with a view to absorbing the Army).

The Salvation Army, however, is not a subdivision of any other structure. We are a free–standing and independent people of God, raised up by Him for the propagation of the gospel of salvation for the whosoever, for the living of holy lives and for the alleviation of human suffering in the name of Jesus Christ, according to the means and resources at our disposal.

I maintain that the Army cannot rightly or fully be understood in modern times unless seen as a worldwide evangelical Christian church (as well as a human service agency, and in many parts of the world, including the United States, as a non–profit corporation).

Historical Development

If we could turn back the clock and sit down with the Army's founder, William Booth, to discuss whether he saw the Army as a church, we might get a different point of view. Even though I take the clear view that we are, at this point in our history, a church, I recognize that Salvationists have not always seen themselves this way. John Coutts said this: "Booth became the founder of a new denomination, while believing—like most founders of new denom-inations—that he was doing nothing of the kind."[1]

It is fascinating to note the Army's changing self–perceptions down through the years. One seminal document is *The Salvation Army in Relation to the Church and State* published in 1889. It is a collection of public speeches by Catherine Booth, wife of William and intellectual powerhouse of the early Salvation Army. Speaking in London in March 1883 on the relation of the Army to the churches, she at no point says unambiguously that the Army is a new church body. Rather, she wanted to show that the Army was "one in aim with the churches" and "not diverse from the churches in the great fundamental doctrines of Christianity."[2]

William Booth, in withdrawing from his ministry within Methodism, did not perceive himself as thereby withdrawing from the church. Catherine too felt a close kinship between the Army and the churches, but still regarded Salvationists as distinct from the churches. The Army was not one of the churches. She offered no classification of the movement her husband commanded. It was as though both of them saw the Army as *sui generis*, a thing apart, the only one of its kind, incapable of being fitted into any pre–existing category. What was the Army? The Booths would have said, "It is the Army!" No need was felt, in those halcyon and pioneering days, of saying anything more.

Several generations later, General Arnold Brown asked his scholarly predecessor, Frederick Coutts, to rearticulate our stance in relation to the church. In *The Salvation Army in Relation to the Church,* Coutts reflects upon the nature of the true church. By this he means the mystical and spiritual fellowship of all true believers upon the Lord Jesus Christ, the "household of faith," the one true and universal church as "the bride of Christ."[3] He argues for what must have even then been obvious, that The Salvation Army is part of the body of Christ. He opens with this statement: "The purpose of this brief study is to reaffirm what has so often been stated in the course of our history, namely, that of 'the Great Church' of the Living God, we claim, and have ever claimed, that we of The Salvation Army are an integral part and element—a living fruit-bearing branch in the True Vine. And such we pray that God may ever keep us."[4]

No doubt this statement needed reaffirming in 1978, but it still falls short of answering directly the question of whether or not The Salvation Army is a church. Exactly what sort of thing is the Army? It is an organization, a movement, a mission to the unconverted, a social agency, a vast worldwide enterprise, an Army on the march for Christ. But can it be said to be a church?

A Church?

In some parts of the world, any such suggestion might bring a look of disbelief from even our closest friends and advisors. This is not altogether their fault. Sometimes (let's admit it!) we have been too reticent, or too muddle–headed in our thinking or simply too inward–looking to realize there is a positive need to spell out *all* there is to tell about who and what we really are. Happily, there is ample historical evidence that the Army has never been totally removed from the self–perception of being a church. Back in 1900, the Annual Report of The Salvation Army in Boston was entitled *The Church of the Back Street*.[5] There it is, an open self–identification by the Army at the turn of the century as a church, and in a fundraising document at that!

In 1957, the USA Commissioners' Conference issued a *Definitive Statement of Salvation Army Services and Activities in the USA*. This publication was reissued four times before 1989. In it a Salvation Army corps is defined as "the church home of Salvationists" and Salvation Army soldiers as "those who make The Salvation Army their church home."[6] Again, we have an instinctive linking of the Army and "church."

In 1972, the Commissioners' Conference in the United States published *The Role of the Corps Officer in the USA*. This document does not hesitate to draw a parallel between the structure and purposes of a Salvation Army corps and the church of the New Testament. It makes repeated references to "other churches," clearly implying that the Army is a church in its own right, and goes on to describe the part played by corps officers in local ministerial fellowships in "cooperation with other churches."[7] The vocabulary of the "church" is used throughout this high level document with obvious ease, and with an absence of self–consciousness.

The USA Southern territory's monthly newspaper, *Southern Spirit*, in its September 24, 1998 issue, published an open letter compiled by representative youth of the territory, which was addressed to the territorial commander, Commissioner John Busby. It arose out of the territory's first annual youth forum, held in Atlanta, Georgia. The young Salvationists collated the responses from their small group discussions and framed their open letter to give eloquent expression to their collective inner convictions and hopes. Their first joint commitment, under the heading "Sharing the Army Message," was as follows: "To let others know through uniform wearing, advertising, and direct contact that The Salvation Army is God's Army, an organization, a church, with a lifestyle which promotes personal relationships with Jesus Christ."[8] The rest of the letter builds on this opening assertion that the Army is a church.

Our current international Mission Statement is less certain about all of this, not quite affirming that we are a church in our own right. It begins: "The Salvation Army, an international movement, is an evangelical part of the universal Christian church." Many territories around the Army world have adopted this statement as it stands or in a slightly modified form, even though it falls short of saying directly that we are a church. The reasons for this reticence are not immediately obvious, and many within our ranks are looking now for something a little more precise. They are asking: "If we are just a 'part' of something else, what sort of 'part' are we?" They were rewarded by the publication in 1998 of *Salvation Story*, the new Salvation Army *Handbook of Doctrine*. *Salvation Story* is an international publication approved by the General of The Salvation Army and compiled by the International Doctrine Council. Chapter 10 deals with the doctrine of the church and contains this statement at its outset: "The Church is the fellowship of all who are justified and sanctified by grace through faith in Christ ... Salvation Army doctrine requires a doctrine of the Church. Each doctrine begins 'We believe ....' 'We' points to a body of believers, a community of faith—a church."[9] At last! There it is! An official Army publication, sanctioned at the highest level, telling all who read it that the Army is a church. This is much more specific, and ecclesiologically more self–assured, than saying vaguely that we are "part of" the "universal Christian church," though in itself this assertion is important. The new *Handbook* offers no hedging, no equivocation, no ambiguity— just a plain and simple assertion: the Army is a church.

However, saying it is so does not make it so. There are still those who would say that no matter how often or how loud the Army says it is a church, it is mistaken. So, let us examine the question from three different points of view: the theological, the sociological and the legal. How would a theologian answer the question of whether the Army is a church? What would a sociologist say about it? And what would a lawyer's answer be?

The Theological Approach

What are the authenticating marks of a true church? Let us take two ancient creeds of the church, the Apostles' Creed and the Nicene Creed, and base our criteria on these. Together they show the following to be the marks of a true church:

- The church is one.
- The church is holy.
- The church is catholic.
- The church is apostolic.

How then does The Salvation Army measure up to these tests? We are truly *one* with all other believers. All who acknowledge Jesus as Lord are seen as brothers and sisters in Christ by Salvationists all around the world. We can find true fellowship with any such person. Our oneness, our solidarity in Christ, stems not from belonging to the same formal structure or to the same denomination, but from our common faith in Jesus as Lord and as our Redeeming Savior. This is the one true church of which Frederick Coutts wrote. It is the "body of Christ." Salvationists are part of this body by reason of their personal faith and trust in Jesus. This body is one body, even though its unity is not always made visible. In this sense the Army is one with all other true churches and Christian believers.

A true church is also a *holy* church. In the New Testament all believers are described as "holy" or as "saints," meaning that because of their acceptance of Jesus as Lord they have now been set aside for His service and to live to His glory. We are called by God to be holy individuals bound together in a faith community, a church. Salvationists believe this and actively teach and preach it. We state in our formal doctrines "that it is the privilege of all believers to be wholly sanctified and that their whole spirit and soul and body may be preserved blameless unto the coming of our Lord Jesus Christ."[10] We assert this not for Salvationists alone, but for all who truly accept Jesus as their Savior from sin. We are, in this way, a holy church at one with other holy churches and together forming one holy body of Christ on earth.

The ancient creeds tell us that the true church is *catholic*. Here catholic simply means universal. To say "I believe in the holy catholic church" is to declare a belief in the whole, united body of Christ on earth made up of all believers regardless of denominational affiliation. It is to affirm one's belief in a church that is loyal and obedient to Christ regardless of time or place. We accept that the one true church of Christ is not parochial or confined by human boundaries. The Salvation Army corps in your town is a local church functioning and witnessing in a particular geographical location. It is, in turn, part of the wider national and international denomination known as The Salvation Army, which can rightly be called a Christian church. The entire Army is part of the universal body of Christ along with all other Christian churches, and indeed along with all other believers upon the Lord Jesus Christ who may not belong formally to any structured denomination. The Army is part of the holy catholic church, being an authentic expression of the body of Christ.

The true church is *apostolic* in that it witnesses to the apostolic testimony concerning Christ. The doctrine, the preaching and the witness of a true church will measure up to the truths of the apostolic proclamation recorded in holy Scripture. The Salvation Army in its formal statement of doctrine places the authority and priority of the Scriptures at the beginning. We regard the Scriptures as the only divine rule of Christian faith and practice. They embody the truth about Christ and the record of the witness of the apostles and of the early church.

On the other hand, it should be noted that the debate among the various denominations as to the nature of apostolic succession in the ordination of priests or ministers is not a part of Salvationist concern. The Army's second General, Bramwell Booth, writing in his *Journal* on April 21, 1921, observed that the early church "seems to have made little of 'ordination' but much of 'appointment.'"[11] Salvation Army officers do not practice the laying on of hands, nor are they themselves commissioned and ordained by this outward symbol. Rather, they receive what has sometimes been called the ordination of the nail–pierced hands. It is Christ who commissions, as He did long ago for the Twelve, and it is He who today ordains for ministry and service in both church and world without the need of any one particular ritual to make that ordination authentic.

Salvationists know and witness therefore that the church (in this context, the body of Christ including The Salvation Army) is one, holy, catholic and apostolic. We can say with our whole hearts that this is so, and that we strive and pray for The Salvation Army to remain true to this calling under Christ the Lord. For this reason the theological answer to the question of whether the Army can rightly be called a church must be in the affirmative.

The Sociological Approach

A sociologist, if asked whether The Salvation Army is a church, would respond by saying, "Well, let's look at the group behavior of Salvationists. You should be able to recognize what they are by the way they act."

> Q: What is the nature of their practice?Do Salvationists gather for worship in a formal setting?
> A: Yes, several times a week and especially on Sunday, the Lord's day.

> Q: Do they engage in prayer together?
> A: Yes, they do.

Q: Do they meet for Christian fellowship on a social basis, either in their buildings or elsewhere?
A: Yes, they do.

Q: Do they use a sacred text?
A: Yes, they do. It is the Bible.

Q: Do they have official memberships and some sort of receiving of believers into their circle of faith?
A: Yes, they do. The believers who come into full adult membership are called "soldiers."

Q: Do they have a separate and recognized spiritual leadership within the group?
A: Yes, they do. These are called "officers."

At this point the sociologist asking the questions will in all likelihood throw up his hands and exclaim, "Enough! I'm convinced! If these folk are not a church, then I cannot think what else they might be! Their behavior tells you all you need to know."

In June 1998, some revealing results were published of a survey conducted in the United Kingdom, the land of the Army's birth.[12] It showed that as much as 50 percent of the public described the Army as a "church," or as a "church with a charity element." Fifty percent may seem high, but we have been ministering with a strong profile in the United Kingdom using the name of The Salvation Army since 1878, so it could have been expected to be higher. Notably, an additional 32 percent described the Army as a "charity with a church element." This description comes close (and of course in many lands the Army is, like many churches, also registered officially as a charity or as a non–profit foundation), but it puts the behavioral cart before the theological horse. Everything we do by way of charitable outreach is done only because we are first a church, with faith convictions that fuel the engine and shape the ethos of our compassionate endeavor.

The Legal Approach

The legal analysis could be the toughest test of all. Theologians or sociologists might not pay too much attention to the opinions of the lawyers, but it is at this point that we see just how much can hang upon the question of whether or not the Army is a church, at least in the eyes of the law. If the Army were not recognized by law as a church in, for example, the United States, it would not have the protection of the legal doctrine of the separation of church and state. Its officers would not be eligible to serve as military chaplains in time of war, and they would not be recognized as prison chaplains, university chaplains or as hospital chaplains. Army personnel would have no place in ecumenical circles. We would be excluded from national ecumenical bodies, from similar bodies at local levels, and our officers would be outsiders to the ministers' fraternals which are found in every community across America.[13]

The lawyer who is asked to give an opinion on whether the Army is a church will first settle upon the legal definition of "church" to see if the Army fits that definition. This exact question arose, not in theory, but in sharp reality as long ago as September 1917. The world was at war, and America had decided to enter the conflict. The Salvation Army in the United States rallied to the cause of the nation, and Army officers applied for military chaplaincies. It fell to the United States War Department to determine whether or not these officers were eligible to hold such positions in the armed forces. On September 12, 1917 a judgment was handed down by the office of the Judge Advocate General in Washington, DC.[14] It is worth quoting from this judgment at length:

> The special qualifications of an Army Chaplain are that he shall be a regularly ordained minister of some religious denomination .... The essential question submitted involves the two following essentials: 1) Is The Salvation Army a religious denomination? 2) Are its ministers regularly ordained as such? In the opinion of this office ... it was substantially held that while the methods of worship of The Salvation Army, as well as

its form of organization, differ from other religious denominations, that such departures are in no sense fundamental, nor do they justify distinguishing The Salvation Army as such; nor would they justify placing it in a different class from that which is usually accorded to other religious denominations. ... It may be said that its General corresponds to its supreme head, that its commissioned officers correspond to the ministers and priests of various grades in other religious organizations, and that its corps correspond to the churches, and its soldiers to the members of the ordinary religious denominations. ... It has a distinct legal existence; a recognized creed and form of worship; a definite and distinct ecclesiastical government; a formal code of doctrine and discipline; a distinct religious history; a membership not associated with any other church or denomination; a complete organization with officers ministering to their congregations, ordained by a system of selection after completing prescribed courses of study. In common with other churches, it has literature of its own; established places of religious worship; regular congregations; regular religious services; and schools for the preparation of its ministers ... [who] perform marriage ceremonies, bury the dead, dedicate children, console the bereaved and advise and instruct the members of their congregations. It is therefore the opinion of this office that The Salvation Army possesses all the elements required for a religious denomination; and that its ministers are regularly ordained within the meaning of the statutes.[15]

Let this be the last word on whether or not the Army is a church! Now we ask, what kind of church?

Chapter 2
Are Salvationists Protestants?

Protestantism • The Centrality of Grace • The Indispensability of Faith • The Role of Scripture • The Priesthood of All Believers • The Holy Life • Protestant Worship

If then a Salvation Army corps is a local church, and the wider international Army is a worldwide church, what kind of church are we talking about? Where does the Army stand on the ecclesiastical spectrum? What does it mean if we say we are "Protestants"?

For some this word conjures up negative images of angry Christians who, ever since the sixteenth century, have declaimed against the Pope and Rome, denouncing them as the Antichrist! This is a cruel caricature of Protestantism. It is true that relationships between Roman Catholics and non–Catholics have often been under enormous stress, and still this can be seen in political struggles, not least in Northern Ireland and the Republic of Ireland. However, it is more important to realize that mutual understanding between Protestants and Catholics has been growing rapidly in the last 35 years or so, ever since the Second Vatican Council in 1964.[1]

Before that watershed event for the whole of the body of Christ, and for the Roman Catholic Church in particular, Protestants were looked upon by Rome (as were Orthodox Christians) as separated brethren whose proper spiritual home was the Roman Catholic Church.[2] Now, however, Rome sees other believers as kindred followers of Jesus Christ with whom rich fellowship can be shared, though perfect communion together is regarded as achievable only within the fold of the Roman Catholic Church. We are therefore now in an era when really significant dialogue is being undertaken between Catholics and many branches of Protestantism. (For example, Rome now feels able to speak of the Church of England as "our sister church," remarkable when it is remembered that Anglicanism was a direct product of the Reformation in England.)[3] This is a hopeful sign for the whole body of Christ on earth as divisions come gradually to be given less prominence than those deep things of the faith we have in common. It is sad that, just occasionally, the old attitudes rear their head. In 1979 a Catholic publishing house in England, Sheed and Ward, issued *A Handbook of Heresies* in which are listed, among others, the following false creeds: Gnosticism, Montanism, Arianism, Nestorianism, and Protestantism! Not a helpful approach! Poor old Martin Luther gets labelled as a "heresiarch," a founder of a heresy.[4] I breathed a sigh of relief on finding that "Salvationism" was not listed!

When Protestants consider Roman Catholicism they see infallible dogmas, rituals carried on in the same way all over the world for many centuries and one single human ruler in the person of the Pope, the Bishop of Rome. Yet we need to grasp that, simply by virtue of the cultural diversity within which Rome functions, the Catholic Church cannot properly be understood unless its immense variety is recognized. We in The Salvation Army can enter into this recognition more readily than some perhaps, for we are at work and in ministry in 106 countries, with one central and unifying office in London, England where the Army's elected international leader, the General of The Salvation Army, is located. The Army is recognizably the Army wherever you may find it, but nowhere is it ever quite the same as anywhere else! So it is for Catholicism, in its infinite variety of cultural settings and expressions.

Protestantism

By contrast, that which goes by the name of Protestantism has never been able to claim one common or central authority, has never had a systematized international structure and has never been a homogeneous whole. From the outset of the sixteenth century Reformation in Europe, there were many different intellectual leaders across the continent, each with a special doctrinal emphasis and each emerging from a distinctive ecclesiastical and political culture. We can think of Martin Luther, Philip Melanchthon, Ulrich Zwingli, John Calvin and others. From their time to the present day it has made more sense to speak of "Protestantisms" rather than using the term in the singular and thereby perpetuating the myth that this branch of Christianity is one simple thing, easily encompassed.

A glance around the Protestant scene in North America will confirm this. Here we see modern expressions of the Reformation very different from those of European Protestantism. Each has its own specific history in America. We have the Pilgrim Fathers (British Calvinists) landing on the east coast in 1620 at what is now known as Plymouth, Massachusetts. The Church of England was established as an official church in the original thirteen colonies, but then came the influence of the Virginia Baptists and the separation of church and state. The successful War of Independence severed the link between the Anglicans (Episcopalians) and England (specifically in the cessation of ordinations of colonial clergy by the Bishop of London), giving way to the rise of the Baptists and Methodists. Today the largest Christian community in the United States is the Southern Baptists, followed by the United Methodist Church and the National Baptist Convention, an African–American church. The Lutherans are strong, but segmented, as in 1987 the majority came together in the Evangelical Lutheran Church, the minority remaining the Lutheran Church—Missouri Synod. The United Church of Christ is the result of a merger nearly thirty years ago among Congregationalists. It is of the Calvinist tradition, but the Presbyterians, also from that background, remain distinct. All of these are American Protestant churches, together weaving a rich but variegated, complex tapestry.[5]

Before analyzing The Salvation Army's place in all of this, it may be useful to deal with two mistaken ideas of Protestantism.

First, the name itself. The word comes from the Latin, *protestari*, meaning "to witness, to testify." It does *not* mean "to protest." The name of "Protestants" was first used by a group of Lutherans about themselves in the 1529 Imperial Diet (Parliament) of Speyer in Germany. They *attested* (testified or witnessed) to the absolute reliability of the Scriptures. "It can never fail us or deceive us," they declared. The notion of protesting or denouncing, or attacking in negative terms some other church's creed is not a part of historic Protestantism. True, in witnessing to our convictions, we might be perceived as being in disagreement with the beliefs of others. That seems to me to be unavoidable, but the primary intention should always be to speak positively about our own stance, and always charitably about the positions of others. My dear Mother used to tell her children, "I am an Irish Protestant, which means I am an *attestant* to deeply held truths." It is an important point.

A second common mistake is to caricature the essence of Protestantism as simply regarding each believer as having the right of private judgment in matters of the spiritual life. No one having a grasp of the lives and teachings of the Reformers would make this mistake. They saw themselves reaching back through the years, leap–frogging as it were, to rediscover the genuine faith of the church as it was without the accretions of the dogmas of medieval Catholicism. There was little stress upon individualism. Instead much was said and written about the church as a community of the faithful and her need to be pure in obedience to Christ. It was not a matter of telling people that they could conveniently invent their own gospel. Rather the message was the need for each individual to make up his or her own mind about the claims of Christ upon them. Would those claims be accepted and responded to? This was the key question. The Reformers taught that the church cannot do this for us. It is not efficacious to say, "I will let the church do my believing for me." That is an abdication of personal responsibility. A personal embracing of salvation in Christ was and still is the irreducible minimum.

Let us consider some broad characteristics of Protestantism, the great common themes and emphases of the Protestant attestation, to see whether The Salvation Army shares them.

The Centrality of Grace

There is no more important word in the Protestant vocabulary than "grace." It is the grace of our Lord Jesus Christ. It is the loving and undeserved favor of God shown to us in the person of Jesus. In Romans 5:8, we are told that God showed His love for us "in that while we were yet sinners Christ died for us." So grace is not a "thing," but is God giving us Himself in Christ. The Old Testament speaks of God's loving–kindness, His steadfast love, while the New Testament stresses His mercy and forgiveness. Grace is also empowerment for right living. In 2 Corinthians 12:9 we read: "My grace is sufficient for you, for My power is made perfect in weakness." All this is absolutely at the heart of Salvationist belief and witness. Our eighth Article of Faith states: "We believe we are justified by *grace* through faith in our Lord Jesus Christ and that he that believeth hath the witness in himself."[6] The *Songbook of The Salvation Army* abounds in hymns and choruses of grace and faith, with over 270 occurrences of the word "grace" in evidence.[7]

The Indispensability of Faith

In common with the Reformers, Salvationists understand faith as a personal trust in Jesus and obedience to His teachings in the Scriptures. It is not a mere intellectual assent to statements about God. Martin Luther saw faith as a lively, reckless confidence in the grace of God. Here grace and faith are linked, as in the Article of Faith quoted above. They go together like "love and marriage," or as the once popular song said, like a "horse and carriage." All of this is in keeping with the Army's understanding and practice.

The Role of Scripture

Protestants proclaim the primacy of Scripture in matters of faith. Unlike Roman Catholics, we do not regard the traditions of the church as having equal authority with Scripture. Article One of The Salvation Army's doctrines states that nothing but the Scriptures can be regarded as "the divine rule of Christian faith and practice."[8]

They are divinely inspired, are thus authoritative and are their own best interpreter. Through them, the Holy Spirit continues to speak to the churches. Summing up the Army's entire doctrinal position, our new *Handbook of Doctrine* (*Salvation Story*) says, "We hold a faith that finds its definition and defense in Scripture."[9] This is a splendid, succinct way of putting it. To define our faith, to determine its substantive content, we look to Scripture. We can accept nothing inconsistent with Scripture and rely upon Scripture to articulate all we preach and teach. Further, the Bible is also the defense of our faith. We rely upon it when we are under criticism, greeted with scepticism or told we are deluded. It is the primary source for the apologetics of our faith.

Salvationists are therefore a people of the Book. We believe that God, through His actions, has made known to us what we could never discover for ourselves—His loving character, saving power, and eternal purposes. His self–revelation is reliably preserved and presented in the living record of holy Scripture. This revelation is centered in the person of Jesus Christ, whom Scripture tells us is the living Word of God.

This primary and overriding emphasis upon the Scriptures ought not to be misunderstood. Salvationists are not bibliolaters. We do not worship the Bible. We worship the triune Godhead shown in God the Father, God the Son and God the Holy Spirit. The Bible is but the means by which God reveals to us the truths He wants us to know and live by. We respect it. We take it very seriously indeed. We bring to bear upon it our God–given intellects and our powers of reason. We do not treat it or what is written in it in some mindless manner. We do not make of it a superstition. We are aware and knowledgeable about the fruits of contemporary scholarship and theological reflection, but we do not feel we need to accept all theories or opinions, for some are mutually exclusive! We are discriminating with regard to academic pronouncements upon the origins or reliability of the Scriptures. We recognize that much that is scholarly serves to enhance our understanding of the Bible's message and its application in modern times, but we do not feel obliged to endorse any approach that detracts from our belief in the divine inspiration of the Scripture and its consequent authority in matters of faith.

Perhaps it ought to be mentioned here that within the ranks of Salvationists there is a tiny minority, mostly among the officers, who see themselves as "liberals" in matters theological. Most, but not all, of these are found outside North America, and not a few in the United Kingdom. They present themselves as in tune with, and knowledgeable about, modernist scholarship and can occasionally be heard to classify colleagues who show a more discriminating approach as "conservative."

The truth is that there are no real liberals in The Salvation Army. Consider how this term is used in the wider world of academic theology. It is taken to indicate those at one far extreme of the theological spectrum, those capable of viewing the Bible as no more than helpful literature or a collection of myths and lifestyle–inspiring stories, or those who are in holy orders but deny a belief in the existence of a personal deity, reject the relevance of the moral teaching of the Scriptures for the twentieth and twenty–first centuries, and generally hold that there are no spiritual or theological certainties.

It is hardly sensible, therefore, for any officer of The Salvation Army to apply a "liberal" label to himself or herself or any other colleague. Equally, it is unproductive, occasionally even hurtful, to seek to categorize others as "conservative." In terms of the theological and ecclesiastical spectrum mentioned earlier, *all* Salvation Army officers are conservatives, and it does no good to try to use the vocabulary or classifications of academia while attaching to them some private alternative meaning. Let us simply be ourselves and take pleasure in the occasional difference of emphasis. That way we learn from one another, instead of dismissing one another too easily with pseudo–intellectual epithets.

What then is meant by the inspiration and authority of the Bible? When the Army speaks of the divine inspiration of the Bible we mean that these writings are the gift of God to us and not our own human achievement. We recognize an interaction of divine power and human response in bringing these works into being. To quote the *Salvation Story* again: "The precious treasure of revealed truth is communicated and preserved in the earthen vessel of written human language."[10] Using a variety of human sources, the biblical writers, enlightened and directed by the Holy Spirit, produced a wholly reliable and trustworthy witness to the saving work of God in Christ. We do not entertain simplistic notions of divine dictation, of humans becoming automata or entering into trances to receive the words they wrote. Neither do we necessarily claim that each and every book in the Bible was produced at one sitting or in one place at one time. We can hold to our view of inspiration and also recognize the possible likelihood that many of the books as we now have them went through a process of development, even through various editorial hands, all of this being miraculously under the providential and guiding hand of Almighty God.

We can discern in the Scriptures individual styles of writing, habits of thought, cultural influences and evidences of human finiteness of knowledge. The writers were free, using their own unique styles and backgrounds. The end product, however, cannot be explained satisfactorily in human terms alone. If the work was that of the human authors, it was even more the work of God. It emanated from the mind and heart of God. No unaided or uninspired human faculties could reveal such wisdom, truth or power. Note that The Salvation Army's statement of faith contains no reference to the infallibility or inerrancy of Scripture. Our claim is that any person can rely utterly upon the Scriptures of both the Old and New Testaments for absolutely reliable instruction and guidance in matters of divine truth and the Christian life, for in the pages of the Bible we encounter the living and risen Christ, who is Himself the Word of God.

To assert that the Bible is the inspired word of God takes us on inevitably to the concomitant belief that it is also authoritative. In common with most other Protestants we recognize, however, that the interpretation of Scripture must be carried on in the context of learning what the church, taken as whole, and through the centuries, has made of it. New insights come with every generation, but our individual exegesis of the Scriptures needs to be measured and tested against the corporate mind of the church in general. This is because we believe that the Holy Spirit is given to the body of Christ on earth corporately as well as to individual Christians. We therefore regard it as necessary to acknowledge three authorities in matters of faith: first, and of overriding importance, are the Scriptures, and nothing opposed to them can be treated as sound for our doctrine; then come the insights about the meaning of the Scriptures that repose in the wider body of Christ and against which we have to test our individual understanding of what we are reading; finally, we have the direct guidance of the Holy Spirit for both the church and the individual believer.

It should now be clear that Salvationists are Bible–believing Christians. We are not fundamentalists in the sense of being unthinking literalists. Rather we approach the Scriptures with a profound and reverential respect, knowing from Whom they have come and to Whom they can unerringly guide us safely home.

The Priesthood of All Believers

The Reformation doctrine of the priesthood of all believers is much referred to, but not always understood. It has come to be a slogan for those who want to say that anyone can do anything within the church. In classical Protestantism it has never meant this and certainly was not used in this way by the Reformers of the sixteenth century.

It is in fact a *via media*, a middle way, between two opposing views of grace and of who is authorized to mediate grace within the body of Christ. One view is that only the church can control grace, dispensing or withholding it at will. This is not a tenet of Protestantism. The opposing view is that grace and the benefits of the gospel can be assimilated independently of the community of faith, as though "privatized" or "individualized" by a believer into some sort of sentimental emotional experience. Neither is this the teaching of Protestantism. Between these two extremes, Protestants, including Salvationists, espouse the doctrine of the priesthood of all believers. It finds its Biblical pedigree in 1 Peter 2:5 where Christian believers are said to be "a royal priesthood" offering "spiritual sacrifices" to God. This is understood to mean that *all* believers, and not only a special priestly class of believers, join Christ in what Scripture describes as His High Priestly work (His perfect, spotless and final self–giving in sacrifice for our sins) by also offering themselves as a living sacrifice—first to God and then to their fellow human beings in self–denying service and witness. Notice that this does not touch directly or explicitly upon the question of who does what in the life and affairs of the church. That issue is entirely a secondary one, being merely an implication of the doctrine and not a part of the doctrine *per se.*

Under the doctrine of the priesthood of all believers, each believer offers himself as a sacrifice according to the pattern laid down by Christ, and all these individual sacrifices are taken up into one perpetual offering made by the one eternal High Priest of the New Covenant. Understood thus, the doctrine does not mean that a Protestant Christian can say: "The Catholics need a priest, but I am my own priest." This is theological nonsense. Neither does it justify the claim: "In my Protestant church anyone can do anything. We do not have to have anyone special to preach or administer communion or bury the dead." The doctrine gives no excuse for the absence of good order in the church. It allows the recognition of distinctive roles for both the laity and the clergy. It implies that both can exercise ministry, each in their own duly appointed spheres (the precise limits of these will vary in detail from denomination to denomination), but that—and this is the key point—the ministry of each is but an aspect of the one ministry that the Holy Spirit inspires and sustains in the church universal.

The Salvation Army believes this doctrine. It is not stated explicitly in our formal Articles of Faith but is assumed, not only in much of our literature, but also in our ordering of local corps (churches) and in our regulations governing that matter. Throughout our history we have given very large and prominent roles to lay Salvationists at a local level. Those taking on specific responsibilities are known as local officers, though they are not ordained or commissioned for full–time service as are officers. A documentary commission is issued to verify their function within the body of believers, and they work under the supervision and pastoral care of the officer in charge of the corps in a given locality. Some non–ordained menbers of the church are allowed to take up wider responsibilities and to carry out the same functions in a corps as an ordained and commissioned officer. I refer here to sergeants, envoys and auxiliary–captains. (In Pakistan we also use the term corps leader for such a person.) The doctrine of the priesthood of all believers gives theological justification for this approach.

We believe the grace that energizes the ordained clergy is the same grace and of the same order as that which empowers and sustains the ministry and service of lay persons. They have offered themselves in the same living sacrifice and are all part of the royal priesthood of believers. Any distinction between them is one of *role or function*, not one of priestly or spiritual status. To put this another way, we do not believe that there is a special, unique or exclusive grace of God available to the ordained person, but unavailable to non–ordained believers.

The Holy Life

Before the Reformation it was customary to think of a truly holy life as being possible only if lived in the closed environment of a convent or monastery. The feasibility of a pure and holy life worked out pragmatically in the maelstrom of the outside, secular world is a legacy of the Reformers. They rejected the notion that to truly please God it was necessary to turn one's back upon the world, abandoning it for the cloister. This approach has come to be known as "dualism," the recognizing of two separate states: one the cloistered life in which, and only in which, a holy life could be achieved; the other the secular world, where Christ could be loved and followed, but only imperfectly obeyed. True holiness, it was said, could not flourish outside the monastery or convent.

The Reformers reassessed the long–held distinction between the sacred and the secular. They taught that all callings are sacred. The calling of the clergyman is no more sacred than that of the school teacher or the tax collector. Martin Luther said that the works of monks and priests are in no way whatever superior in God's sight to a farmer working in a field or a woman looking after her home becuase all of God's children are measured by faith alone. John Calvin agreed that it is not necessary to enter a monastery to serve God, as the whole world is God's monastery.

The Salvation Army has embraced this teaching from its earliest days. It has expressed it in its holiness literature and enshrined it in Article Ten of its formal Doctrines: "We believe that it is the privilege of all believers to be wholly sanctified, and that their whole spirit and soul and body may be preserved blameless unto the coming of our Lord Jesus Christ."[11] This places the Army among those churches which together go by the name of the holiness movement. It is one of The Salvation Army's major distinctives.

We believe and teach that daily, hourly we can live in victory over temptation and sin, being recipients of grace that enables and empowers for holy living and practical purity even in the secular world. Our emphasis upon this was stronger when the Army was young. Today some of the cutting edge of this doctrine has been lost, and we have not been successful in restating it for the modern age. To neglect this as a doctrine of our faith is to risk losing the practical experience, and when that happens the Army languishes. It is still there, deep in the collective Salvationist psyche, more talked about perhaps in North America than in Europe or elsewhere.

The twenty–first century must be one in which the Army faces both the intellectual challenge and the challenge to our own personal spirituality that our historic holiness teaching brings. God will cause to be raised up in our midst those who will refocus us upon these truths, remolding their presentation to the modern age without in any way undermining the great Scriptural insights that gave birth to the holiness movement and injected passion and fervor into the first Salvationists. We are at a point in our history when the grasp of the great John Wesley, of William and Catherine Booth, of Samuel Logan Brengle upon Scriptural holiness and its practical implications for daily living needs to be revisited and revived in a manner that will speak to the millennium generations.[12]

Protestant Worship

God receives as acceptable all sincere worship coming from true hearts, regardless of the denominational setting in which that worship takes place. Worshipping "in spirit and in truth" is what matters.[13] It will not do for one group to gather in church for worship while quietly or inwardly feeling smug toward other groups whose style or content of worship is different. We can be sure God does not smile upon such attitudes. For that reason, what is said next about typical aspects of Protestant worship should not be taken as casting any negative implication upon non–Protestant traditions.

New and experimental forms of worship are to be found all over the world in Protestant churches, including The Salvation Army. This is, as it should be, a very welcome trend. The secret of success as we move into the twenty–first century will be to blend the best of the new with the best of the old. For the moment, I am referring to the more traditional formats of Protestant worship such as prayer, congregational singing, music, Scripture, the sermon, personal giving and testimony to personal experiences of Christ.

All of these are meat and drink to Salvationists and can be seen and heard in Army worship services ("meetings") worldwide. Our prayers are mostly *extempore*, that is, made up on the spot as someone, usually the leader, addresses God aloud from the heart and on behalf of the congregation. Those seated in the congregation also have opportunities to pray aloud with freedom. These prayers might well be accompanied by a softly spoken "Amen" or "Jesus" or some other expression of affirmation and inner assent as the prayer unfolds. Prepared prayers are also used. Salvationists are happy to benefit from the written prayers of others, but we do not have a set liturgy.

The singing of hymns ("songs") and choruses is part and parcel of Army worship. We like to sing with enthusiasm, and we clap our hands frequently, if the rhythm lends itself to that. However, we can change our mood and the meeting's atmosphere quite quickly as the Holy Spirit does His sacred work in the hearts of the leaders and the people. A lively hymn with clapping, brass band accompaniment, and everyone up on their feet, some moving to the music, can soon move into a hushed and solemn moment of adoration as a quiet, reflective chorus is sung or played.

We see the usefulness of singing not only as an expression of praise, not only as a release of spiritual energy, but also as a spiritual discipline. We have learned the value of singing the traditional hymns of Christendom that are packed with doctrinal truth, such as the hymns of the Wesleys, as well as more modern, contemporary choruses and hymns which help us to express our feelings toward the Lord in the language of our day. Salvationist worship reaches its highest heights when both the traditional and the contemporary are given time and space. We must never forget that what is today called "traditional" was once "contemporary," and that what is now "contemporary" will one day be seen as "traditional." Salvationists are, generally speaking, open to anything musical that moves them closer to God in worship. Even if not all among us, especially the younger ones, can understand immediately the words of Charles Wesley or Isaac Newton, we still continue to sing them whole-heartedly, the Holy Spirit gently increasing our insights over time, and in the knowledge that somehow we have been built up and fed thereby, even if we cannot fully explain all that was in the spiritual food! Conversely, the older folk are willing to learn the new songs, sensing clearly that they speak to the hearts of a different generation, but also can quickly come to be a means of grace to believers and worshippers of any age.

No Salvation Army worship service is permitted to take place without the public reading of the Scriptures. Even a musical event or concert must include this in the proceedings. The Scriptures permeate Protestant worship. They are read, recited, sung in Psalms, echoed in prayers and paraphrased in hymns and choruses. Here in Pakistan, where I presently serve, almost all worshippers in an Army meeting carry a Bible, if they are literate. Each Bible is handled with great care and respect. It is not regarded as appropriate to place your Bible on the floor, or even to put another book, for instance your *Songbook,* on top of it.

The preaching of the sermon is still deemed to be a climax to the meeting. All that precedes this is intended to prepare the hearts and minds of the worshippers to hear the Word expounded. What follows the sermon is equally intended to allow an opportunity for reflection and personal response to what has been heard. The place of preaching in the Protestant tradition can be understood by reference to the architectural and interior design of the place of worship. The pulpit is often central, not on the side. In some parts of Scandinavia, the pulpit in Protestant churches is built so high that it allows the preacher to see into the face of every person present, including those in the balcony at the back and sides of the building! The Salvation Army designs the interior of its worship areas so that a platform or rostrum is available for the meeting leader and the preacher. Immediately in front of the platform is the Mercy Seat, a place of private prayer at which the worshipper can kneel in response to the preached message or in order to silently place some inner need before God. Thus the preacher's rostrum and the Mercy Seat form the central focus of the room or auditorium, with the Mercy Seat being clearly visible even from the balcony, the steepness of which will have been determined so that those seated there have a plain view of the preacher and the Mercy Seat. All of this bespeaks the centrality of preaching in the traditions of The Salvation Army.

It is very common indeed for a Salvationist act of worship to include personal testimony. We believe strongly in the effectiveness of personal witness. Sometimes a testimony will be given after preparation, but often the worship service will be opened up for anyone present to stand and share their experience of Christ. At times the response can be slow, perhaps influenced by cultural factors, but often the people will be on their feet in no time at all, eager to speak from their hearts. A wise leader will know when to let this continue, will intuit how the testimonies are enhancing the meeting and edifying the worshippers and will know how to move on seamlessly to the next phase of worship. It is common in Army worship for the prepared meeting plan, or order of service, to be spontaneously adapted to conform to a movement of the Holy Spirit among the worshippers.

All of this shows how much the Army has in union with the

main elements of Protestant worship styles. It ought to be said at this point that most Protestant commentators would add to the features discussed in this chapter some word about the place of sacraments in worship. The distinctive contribution of The Salvation Army to the sacramental dimension will be dealt with in Part Two.

This chapter began by asking if Salvationists are Protestants. The answer is Yes!

Chapter 3
Are Salvationists Evangelicals?

Evangelicalism • The Enlightenment • Scholarship • The Influence of Francis Schaeffer • Salvationist Evangelicalism • Four Great Principles • The Cross and the Mercy Seat • Wesleyan Roots • Three Significant Events

---

The two terms "Evangelicalism" and "evangelism" ought not to be confused. Evangelism is an umbrella word that refers to efforts to spread the gospel, and an evangelist is a person engaged in such work. Evangelicalism, however, is a particular expression of Christianity with its origins in the eighteenth century's Evangelical Revival in England, in which the great John Wesley played so prominent a part. There were several notable movements of the Holy Spirit in the 1700s in which thousands were freshly awakened to the claims of Christ upon them and which resulted in a marked upturn in the moral and spiritual tone of those communities and countries where they occurred. England, Scotland and Ireland were affected, as was North America.

Out of this came Methodism. In turn came the Methodist New Connexion in which the young William Booth ministered. From this emerged The Christian Mission, the immediate forerunner of The Salvation Army. Salvationists therefore have their ecclesiastical roots firmly in the soil of Evangelicalism.

Evangelicalism

Evangelicalism today is the great informal network of Protestant churches and organizations that derive from the eighteenth century revivals already mentioned. Its history covers the period from the Wesleys in England and Jonathan Edwards in the United States' New England, down to America's famous Billy Graham, Canada's James Packer and Britain's John Stott. These are just a very few of the outstanding servants of God who have kept alive the flame of Evangelicalism. They emphasized the personal, transforming power of the gospel. Their constant motivation has been that of the original Pietists, a religious movement in Frankfurt, Germany in the late 1600s which was anxious to save orthodox Lutheranism from the dangers of arid formalism. They saw the need for an inner, personal commitment to Christ, a vibrant personal prayer life and the benefits of engaging personally with the Scriptures on a daily basis.

Through the Wesleys, we can trace the line of descent from the German Pietists right down to the present day and the Evangelicalism found in all parts of the world. In 1994 the Oxford University Press published a symposium in which the size and health of the movement was evaluated.[1] According to this survey, the majority of ordinands in the Church of England are evangelicals, and in Canada the majority of Protestant worshippers on a Sunday are in evangelical churches. In the United States, information from the University of Michigan's Center for Political Studies shows that evangelicals represent 33 percent of the entire American population. It also reports that of all Roman Catholics and Protestants taken together, evangelicals comprise 38 percent of the numerical total. Of Christian believers who attend church regularly, no fewer than 43 percent are in the evangelical tradition.[2]

The discussion of Protestantism offered in chapter 2 tries to demonstrate that, despite its variety of manifestations, there are certain broad emphases that allow us to take a bird's eye view of the movement and to recognize a Protestant church when we encounter one. It is the same with Evangelicalism. It manifests itself in a variety of forms and settings, but has overriding doctrinal concerns that unite all evangelicals to a greater or lesser degree.

The single most significant concern is an insistence on the essential nature of the personal and experiential dimension of the Christian faith. The Reformation's first zeal did not endure with the same intensity forever. Some Lutheran and Reformed churches, a hundred years after the Reformation, found themselves highly formalized. Some of their members reacted also against what they regarded as intellectual excesses of rationalistic orthodoxy, in which the power of human reason was elevated above revelation, subjecting the latter to the judgment of the former. Put another way, "head knowledge" was crowding out "heart knowledge."

The Enlightenment

Closely linked to all this was the later response of Evangelicalism to the fruits of the so–called "Enlightenment," the European intellectual movement of the late seventeenth and eighteenth centuries, influenced by philosophers like France's Rene Descartes and England's John Locke, and by the great English physicist and mathematician, Sir Isaac Newton, the most celebrated physicist before Albert Einstein. Evangelicalism, to be properly understood, needs to be seen against this setting. At its core this movement had a belief in reason, the power of the mind, as the key to human progress and knowledge. It denied our need of a Savior. Starting in Europe, its influence spread widely. In Germany it is associated with thinkers such as Emmanuel Kant and Johann Goethe, the poet and dramatist. In France its most famous sons were the writer Voltaire and the philosopher Jean–Jacques Rousseau. These men propagated radical social and religious views, stressing the basic goodness of human nature and the ultimate capacity of the human race to work out its own salvation. Man could be his own savior! Some of these ideas, together with the Enlightenment's criticism of government and of the church, served to fuel revolutionary thinking in both France and America. Thomas Jefferson, third President of the United States, and Thomas Paine both came under the influence of this thinking. Paine, who was in fact an Englishman, emigrated to America in 1774 and laid the influential groundwork for the Declaration of Independence in his 1776 pamphlet *Common*

Sense. In later writings, such as *The Age of Reason,* he openly attacked classical Christianity.

This brief overview of the Enlightenment reveals just why evangelical Christians would feel out of step with the major thrusts of these thinkers. Many of them were brilliant, but they were also wrong when it came to matters of the soul. Evangelicals have committed themselves to a belief that all have sinned and fallen short of the glory of God and are thus in need of a Savior. Therefore we cannot accept that all human beings are essentially good and can save themselves. If we have come to see the wonder of the self–revelation of God in the person of Jesus of Nazareth and in the pages of holy writ, we shall not want to receive uncritically a view that elevates human reason and rationality above revelation. We shall seek to maintain our belief that reason is but one way to come to truth and that there are truths too deep for reason alone to penetrate. Some truths we know only because God has chosen to reveal them to us. After that, He fully expects us to bring our human faculties of heart and mind to bear upon His revelation. He wants us to grasp all that He offers, not only with a limited part of our beings but with all that we have and are, including our intellects. When rationalists or modernists sometimes say that evangelicals have abandoned their intellects they could not be more wrong. God has given us our gifts of mind. They are to be used with full rigor, and doing so does *not* inescapably lead to the conclusion that faith and spirituality, that religion and personal devotion to a personal God, are irrational pursuits.

Scholarship

Evangelicalism is still wrestling with these issues. Even today some feel threatened by the fruits of scholarship. There is no need for this. All knowledge is God's, but not all theories or opinions are God's. We must go on discerning carefully between knowledge and opinion. We have nothing to fear from scholarly research into the origins and nature of the Scriptures. The Bible can and does withstand all analysis of it. No researcher, no academic, no skeptic, no rationalist can finally undermine God or His Word, which stands forever. Do not let us ever think that terms like "evangelical" and "scholarly" are mutually exclusive. In fact, the reverse is true. It is a very powerful and effective approach to things Christian to be both evangelical and scholarly. This combination looks for warmth of heart, humility of spirit and keenness of mind. It combines in telling fashion a sense of what God requires from us personally and what He can do through an intellect surrendered to His gracious, sanctifying touch.

So it is that a great many evangelicals, including Salvationists, are found today in the world of academia. They have influential roles also in cultural life, in politics, in the labor movements and of course in missionary endeavor. In saying this, it is not meant to suggest that Evangelicalism is the only authentic way to be a Christian. It is that those of us who gladly apply the "evangelical" epithet to ourselves wish to uphold the best insights of the Reformation, together with a recognition of the timeless need to place before anyone willing to listen the possibility of knowing Jesus Christ as Savior in a personally transforming friendship. These goals do not make all evangelicals anti–intellectual, though some have been guilty of this. Neither do they cut us off from other strains of Christianity, though some have behaved exclusively, not least toward the Church of Rome.

At its best, modern Evangelicalism will eschew any form of virulent anti–Catholicism, or any attempt to cruelly stereotype believers from other traditions. In fact we are now seeing certain attempts at genuine conversation between evangelicals and Roman Catholics. One such attempt is happening in Los Angeles and is focusing on practical ways of seeing each other's point of view, through reaching out to young people and sharing speakers at youth events. Another initiative involves shared ministry to Hispanic communities. In describing these, Richard J. Mouw, president of Fuller Theological Seminary, acknowledges that there are many real differences between the participants, but explains his conviction that polarization is often due simply to a lack of information about the other person's outlook and beliefs.[3] For example, he thinks that evangelicals do not fully appreciate the Catholic emphasis upon the doctrine of the church, and Catholics fail equally to grasp the centrality for evangelicals of the doctrine of salvation. When Catholics think ecclesiologically (church), and evangelicals think soteriologically (salvation), they usually finish up talking past each other. He uses as an illustration the Catholic practice of praying to the saints. Evangelicals suspect this waters down the place of Christ through whom we should make all prayers. Catholics respond by explaining that when praying to the saints they are not praying in expectation that these prayers will save them. These are not salvific prayers, but rather a reflection of the Catholic's broad view of the fellowship of the church. It is an ecclesiological emphasis, while evangelicals start from a soteriological emphasis.

Salvationists welcome any interaction that makes for deeper mutuality of understanding between differing traditions. We warm to opportunities to be in contact with Christians from other denominations, whether of the evangelical persuasion or not, for we have long ago learned (and this will become more and more meaningful in the twenty–first century) that the path to closer affinity lies first and foremost in learning to trust other individual believers, even if we have not yet learned fully to trust their ecclesiastical institutions. If we find grace to obey the New Commandment of Christ and love one another with a Christlike love, regardless of denominational affiliation, regardless of historical heritage, we shall all the sooner let the unbelievers see and know that we are all the disciples of Christ.[4]

The Influence of Francis Schaeffer

Let us bring all this down to earth with a short review of the life and work of one of the greatest evangelicals of the twentieth century. I refer to Francis Schaeffer, whose motives and emphases were strikingly similar to those of The Salvation Army. In working through his own personal spiritual crisis in 1952, he concluded that belief must travel hand–in–hand with demonstrative, practical love. (This is very "Salvation Army," though of course Schaeffer was never formally linked to the Army.) This insight is not exclusive to Schaeffer (or to Evangelicalism). In his earlier years, Schaeffer had been so devoted to advocating and validating the academic and propositional truths of his faith that he had neglected his spirit in building up the muscles of his mind. Demonstrative, practical love had been neglected. That which is best in Evangelicalism balances both mind and spirit. So too does the best in Salvationism.

Many thinking and widely read Salvationists of my own generation will gratefully acknowledge being affirmatively influenced by the writings of Francis Schaeffer. It is always a liberating and affirming experience to discover that there beats a heart in tune with our own, but far outside the organizational confines of our church. Educated in the United States at Westminster Seminary, Schaeffer pastored Bible Presbyterian churches for nine years before leaving for Switzerland in 1948 under the auspices of the Presbyterian Independent Board for Foreign Missions. With his wife, Edith, Schaeffer was to establish an independent ministry organization called *L'Abri*, or "The Shelter." Launched on a small scale in 1955 in the Swiss mountains, this community grew to worldwide fame, attracting thousands of visitors from all over the world. It catered mainly to young students who found there an opportunity to explore the world of ideas through informal dialogue with Schaeffer and others, and the chance to discover that their Christian faith could make sense and have explicit relevance to all of life—to culture, morality, politics and philosophy.

Schaeffer, with his Salvationist–like balance of faith and practical compassion, was perhaps the most influential evangelical of the post–World War II years. He clung tenaciously to the inerrancy of the Scriptures. He rejected as pitiful the modern post–Christian approach to truth that sought to distinguish between types of truth: religious, scientific, emotional, psychological, etc. Religious truth and material truth were not two separate realities (he differed from the great theologian Karl Barth about this) for truth is a unity and Christianity speaks only of what Schaeffer called "true truth." He attacked modern culture as expressed in literature, art and film. He took it apart piece by little piece to demonstrate its aridity for the human soul.

He observed young people coming to The Shelter in the Alps

with only their existentialist literature to explain the world to them. He agonized over their emotional and spiritual deprivation. They had been taught in their universities that their lives were the product of chance and that the only real world was what you could touch, see, smell and hear. They had been made to think that there were no moral or religious certainties, that relativism (the theory that there are no absolutes in anything, no enduring moral laws, no lasting or eternally true spiritual insights) was all. He observed their inability therefore to distinguish right from wrong, or to find meaning in their own lives. He resented what had been done to them by agnostic intellectuals or by modernistic theologians to consign them to moral confusion and to inject into them a sense of alienation from their own societies. Their search for something better stirred the compassion of both Edith and Francis Schaeffer, and aroused their anger too. How William and Catherine Booth would have approved these spontaneous responses!

In his first and now famous book, *The God Who Is There*, Schaeffer comes to grips with the arts and with science, challenging their unproven and irrational assumption that human beings are the chance product of an impersonal and material universe.[5] If this were true, then whence personality, whence hope, whence purpose and significance, whence love, morality, beauty, whence the innate power of the spoken and written word? Without Christianity, the human race is left with a choice of only two paths: escapism into mysticism, often facilitated by drugs, or alternatively, a descent into barbarism that reduces and debases humans into mere machines, good for labor, for reproduction, for spare parts and for fighting the wars of the politically ambitious, but inept.

Later, this sharp antipathy to a materialistic view of human life came to be expressed in Schaeffer's fierce opposition to abortion. This drew him into American politics and an affiliation with the pro–life advocates belonging to the conservative right of the Republican Party, something that surprised his earlier devotees who had agreed with him when he had urged that the gospel of Jesus Christ could not be equated with political or even patriotic sentiment. He had even gone so far as to suggest that evangelicals should remove the American flag from their sanctuaries! Not many, if any, did this. Certainly The Salvation Army in the United States did not. To see the national flag standing paired with the Army flag in Salvationist places of worship all over America serves as a constant and eloquent reminder that the divine truths symbolized by the Army's Trinitarian colors—its blue, red and yellow representing respectively Father, Son and Holy Spirit—hold a hope and a message for each and every citizen whose allegiance is pledged to the national emblem. It is a visible statement about the direct relevance of the Army's doctrines and ministry to the lives of everyone in America. (Since leaving America, I have discovered that the Army here in Pakistan often follows the same practice in its worship halls.)

Many books and lectures followed the publication of *The God Who Is There*. Even as far away as the Murree Christian School in northern Pakistan his books could be found and read, courtesy of a 1971 visit by Youth with a Mission. Writing in *Christianity Today*, Michael Hamilton describes Schaeffer as "Evangelicalism's most important public intellectual in the twenty years before his death." He goes on to say that Francis Schaeffer "reshaped American Evangelicalism." Thus, Hamilton concludes:

> *Perhaps no intellectual save C. S. Lewis affected the thinking of evangelicals more profoundly; perhaps no leader of the period save Billy Graham left a deeper stamp on the movement. Together the Schaeffers gave currency to the idea of intentional Christian communities, prodded evangelicals out of their cultural ghetto, inspired an army of evangelicals to become serious scholars, encouraged women who chose roles as mothers and homemakers, mentored the leaders of the New Christian Right, and solidified popular evangelical opposition to abortion.*[6]

Salvationist Evangelicalism

This look at the influence of Francis Schaeffer affords an

opportunity to highlight similarities in Salvationist Evangelicalism. We may never in our literature have been as dogmatic concerning the inerrancy of Scripture in all its aspects, and indeed not all evangelicals would align themselves entirely with Schaeffer in the way he treated this doctrine. However, we join him without hesitation in urging the absolute trustworthiness of the Scriptures in matters of faith, and their reliability as a spiritual and moral guide to a life pleasing to God who made us, to His Son who died to save us and to the Holy Spirit who comes alongside moment by moment to see us through.

We also reject the relativism of the modern age. It is simply nonsense to say, "Your truth is truth for you, but my truth is truth for me." It is one of the great lies of our time, pretending that mutually exclusive points of view can both be true. It has made for moral chaos, robbing both ordinary people and those in leadership positions in our societies of the capacity to see clearly between right and wrong. It has led, in some countries, to the emergence of political parties that no longer have a coherent underlying set of principles to motivate their policies and legislative programs. Instead, each decision is made on the basis of expediency and whatever will keep them in power.

It has also produced in certain church circles a loss of nerve in speaking with a prophetic voice on issues of social ethics. Squeezed by relativistic philosophies on one side and by uncertainty about the lasting relevance of Scripture on the other, many churches have settled for an anemic political correctness, which deprives them of the persuasive and authoritative voice they might once have had. Thus, while sin abounds and wrongdoing becomes respectable, God's people too often remain silent, so that over time their God–given aptitude for speaking compassionately but clearly to government, to opinion–makers, to the media, to the populace about the pressing social and moral issues of the day becomes muted and all but lost.

The Salvation Army might just draw from Schaeffer (who would have made a splendid Salvationist) at least two cheers for its public efforts to hold to what the Bible has to teach us about human sexuality, about gender, about the environment, about the sanctity of human life both in its origins and at its endings, about the centrality of family in God's blueprint for our race, about the solidarity of all ethnic groups as children of the one Creator and about the innate dignity of all regardless of educational, social or financial status. He might also warm to our willingness to encounter people just as they are and at their point of need, asking not where they come from or who was their father, but for the sake of and in the name of Jesus asking only, "Where are you hurting? Can I help?" This is the Salvation Army's down–to–earth expression of what Schaeffer called "demonstrative love."

Four Great Principles

Happily we are not, and never have been, alone in any of this. Evangelicals everywhere are driven by such things. As an expression of part of the body of Christ on earth, numerically large and organizationally diverse, they are united in the grand concepts of biblicism, conversionism, activism and crucicentrism. These four pillars characterize and sustain Salvationist Evangelicalism as we enter the twenty–first century. They will be as needed at least as much tomorrow as they are today. Restated these four bastions of the evangelical wing of Christianity are:

- An insistence upon the Bible as the ultimate written authority for Christians
- An emphasis upon an inner and personal (but never stereotypical) conversion experience
- An explicit recognition of the need for active involvement in religious duties, in compassionate (but never patronizing) social service and in wise social action for the eradication of injustices
- An unfailing focus upon the redeeming work of Jesus on the cross of Calvary, without which there is no gospel.

All of these sound a clarion call to Salvationists everywhere. We have tried, by the grace of God, to do our part in the nineteenth and twentieth centuries. If we were honest, we would say that we have seen mixed results. We would say also that anything accomplished has been what God has wrought. The next century, full of the unknown, and targeted already by those forces arrayed against righteousness and purity, will need us to be more faithful than ever before in our history. We still have a part to play for God.

The Cross and the Mercy Seat

If the twenty–first century is to see a movement of the Spirit anything like that of the Evangelical Revival from which Evangelicalism sprang, it will be because we are continuing to preach the cross of Christ. Of all that characterizes evangelicals, whether they are Salvationists or not, it is the centrality of the cross that matters most. An empty cross, a reminder of the risen Lord, is to be found right at the heart of the Salvation Army's crest or logo. Sometimes our other symbols obscure it, sometimes it is depicted so small that it is almost lost from view. There is a parable in these things. But unmistakable and impossible to miss is the Mercy Seat that can be found at the focal point of every Salvation Army place of worship in the world. Travel to any of the 106 countries where the Army can be found, go into any Army hall, any sanctuary, any citadel, any meeting room, and there you will see in front of the preacher's rostrum a place for kneeling. Sometimes known as the Penitent's Form, it represents the entire calling and mission of The Salvation Army under God, namely the facilitation of a meeting between a man, or a woman or a child (we still believe in the openness of children to the things of God) and the living God who made them and loves them so much that He gave them Jesus to prove it. To understand the Army, you must understand the Mercy Seat, for it is our heartbeat. It symbolizes our mission for the saving of souls for an eternity to be spent with Christ.

Far from being the brainchild of William Booth, the Mercy Seat is described in the Old Testament Scriptures in Exodus 25:1–22. The Lord told the Israelites that He would meet them above the slab covering the Ark of the Covenant. This came to be known as the Mercy Seat, a meeting place between God and mankind. Salvationists believe that such an encounter can take place absolutely anywhere and any time, wherever and whenever a person seeks the Lord in sincerity of heart and mind. The place of such a meeting becomes its own Mercy Seat, hallowed because God's real presence is there. The formal Mercy Seat in our buildings is also made holy by its dedication to God for His sacred purposes, but the gracious work of salvation and of sanctification, of the imparting of divine grace, have never been confined to specialized places or to specific items of church furnishings.

Wesleyan Roots

John Wesley used the device of the "altar call" throughout his lifelong preaching ministry. Still preaching from horseback well into his eighties, he regularly called people to come forward and stand or kneel as an indication that they wished their lives to be transformed by the power of God, or that they wished to make some special offering of themselves in closer communion with or service for their Lord. In modern times we have seen this in the great rallies of Billy Graham. The Salvation Army has been doing it ever since its beginnings. The practice is directly attributable to that of Wesley.

We owe much to Wesleyan Methodism, from which came the Methodist New Connexion in 1797. This was a breakaway from the main body of English Methodism that took place over the issue of church government. Those dissenting and who formed the new grouping looked for a greater role in church affairs for the laity. A Salvationist scholar, Dr. Roger Green, in his biography of Catherine Booth, the co–founder of The Salvation Army, writes: "New Connexion Methodism appeared to offer William what he had been looking for in a denomination: a thoroughly Wesleyan theological base, a strong emphasis on revivalism, and a governance that included representation from the laity and preachers alike."[7]

Here again we see the Army's evangelical credentials. Dr. Green draws out with admirable clarity Booth's self–acknowledged debt to John Wesley: his desire not only to make sinners good, but to ground the saints in a good grasp of sound doctrine; the value of effective visitation in the homes of the members; the place of classes of systematic instruction of the believers; his organizational methods based on democratic committees and voting conferences (Booth came to abandon these because much valuable time was found to be spent in unprofitable debate, but today many alternative consultative mechanisms are in use); and, most vital of all, his embracing of Wesley's doctrine of sanctification by grace, which he simplified but which is still recognizably the child of Wesleyan holiness teaching and is stated in the Army's tenth Doctrine.[8]

Three Significant Events

The first three months of 1998 saw three events taking place that reaffirmed and reinforced the links between The Salvation Army and other evangelicals. In February the international Salvation Army was received into associate membership of the World Evangelical Fellowship (WEF). This body grew out of a gathering of leading evangelicals which was held in London, England, in 1846, and was perpetuated in many countries by the name of the Evangelical Alliance. The Army has maintained membership in these national groups over many years. In 1951 an International Convention of Evangelicals met in Holland, and from this the WEF was born. With its headquarters in Singapore, it embraces 150 million evangelicals in 112 national and regional fellowships, representing more than 600,000 churches. Today the WEF is seen by many as the primary movement for visible global unity among evangelicals.[9]

In March 1998 the biennial meeting of the Lausanne Committee for World Evangelization took place in Toronto. The Committee dates from the 1974 call by Dr. Billy Graham to Christian leaders to meet and consider the evangelical challenges of the age. This resulted in 2,700 participants from 150 countries and the production of the Lausanne Covenant, a statement expressing an evangelical consensus on the meaning and purposes of evangelization (and now forming an Appendix in the Army's new Handbook of Doctrine, *Salvation Story*.) In Toronto, the then Lt. Colonel Earl

Robinson, Secretary for International External Relationships at International Headquarters, was appointed as a member of the Lausanne Executive Committee.[10]

Article 5 of the Lausanne Covenant deals with "Christian Social Responsibility." Evangelicals have sometimes struggled to find a balance between evangelism on the one hand and social service or social action on the other. The Lausanne Covenant sees each as an integral part of the other, a view long espoused by Salvationists. It was thus a very fitting moment when, in February 1998, General Paul Rader visited the Roberts Wesleyan College in Rochester, New York and there dedicated the new Master of Social Work program, the first such degree to have at its center soundly evangelical Christian values and beliefs. On this occasion, General Rader and his wife, Commissioner Kay Rader, received honorary degrees.[11]

These three cameo events, perhaps especially the first two, reveal again the Salvationist desire to be identified with Evangelicalism as a worldwide movement and also to strengthen our relationships in local evangelical fellowships. Simultaneously, however, it needs to be understood that we are equally comfortable in mainstream and more traditional ecumenical circles, often being able to bridge those traditions which still feel mutual wariness toward one another.

Where then have we reached in articulating the place occupied by The Salvation Army on the ecclesiastical spectrum? Earlier chapters established that the Army is a Protestant church, and now it can clearly be seen that within Protestantism, Salvationists stand in the evangelical tradition. We are Protestant evangelicals, but bring to the ecumenical table a willingness to be in fellowship with all who worship Jesus as Lord. In that spirit we can both give and receive, both feed and be fed, be both ourselves and accept others with charity and openness.

Part II
Salvationists as Sacramentalists

Three Moments

1971: I was 26 and had been teaching law at the Inns of Court School of Law in London for a couple of years, when an opening came up in the law faculty at the University of Bristol in the west of England. It was a faculty with a good reputation and the competition among students to be accepted there was intense. So I took the job as a junior member of the teaching staff, commuting every few days the long drive between our home in London and the small suite of rooms I occupied in Badock Hall, a student residence on the University campus. Helen had a teaching job in London, and so moving permanently to Bristol was out of the question. Our bright red, convertible sports car was a very great blessing in those days as it gobbled up the miles between Bristol and London!

I soon discovered that several of the students residing in Badock Hall, for whom I had a counselling responsibility (this was the price of my three–room suite!) had come into personal knowledge of Jesus Christ as their Savior because of a campus evangelical initiative a few months before. It seemed natural to offer them my fairly spacious main room for a weekly get–together where they could read and discuss the Scriptures and spend time in prayer for the many people and situations that burdened their hearts.

On one such occasion, a postgraduate student who had been a committed Christian longer than the others brought up the subject of the sacraments. The discussion ranged freely, and I felt it best to let it follow its own course. I listened intently to these young men exchanging ideas and seeking a firmer grasp upon the things of their new–found faith. Suddenly, the postgraduate looked across at me and said: "You are a Salvationist. Why are you anti–sacraments?"

He had clearly been misinformed about the teaching of The Salvation Army concerning the sacramental life.

1976: Much had happened since Bristol. We had offered ourselves for a lifetime of service as officers of The Salvation Army, feeling beyond a shadow of a doubt that this was the will of God for our lives. We resigned our jobs. To burn my bridges behind me, I sold all my law books. Two years later we were lieutenants, being asked by the Army's International Headquarters if we were willing to take an appointment in Africa. We were, and so in January 1975, after two weeks at sea and three days and nights on a train from Cape Town to Salisbury (now Harare), we reached the Mazowe Secondary School in Rhodesia (now Zimbabwe). Our 22–month–old son, Matthew, toddled inquisitively around our new home, a handsome bungalow with Swedish pinewood ceilings.

We spent Easter 1976 visiting the Kariba Dam with Matthew and his new baby sister, Jenny. We peered across the mighty Zambezi River into Zambia, entry to which was denied us due to the closure of the border because of United Nations sanctions imposed against the Rhodesian government of that day.

There is at Kariba a beautiful, although simply designed, interdenominational church. It has low side walls, allowing a view beyond the sanctuary. With my friend and fellow officer, Allister Lewis, I attended the Easter morning service. Every pew was packed with worshippers. The visiting Anglican priest presided over Holy Communion, explaining that any member of any Christian church would be welcome to receive communion. He placed no particular theological slant on the ceremony. I had never taken communion before. After all, I was a Salvationist and accepted wholeheartedly everything entailed in Salvationist sacramentalism. This left me free to follow the prompting of the Holy Spirit when attending other churches where communion was celebrated.

I moved quietly forward with Allister. We had played a lot of squash together, had got into occasional scrapes together, had always laughed a lot together, and now he was my co–recipient of grace as we remembered the Lord and all that He had done for us.

I was glad that I went forward, but even as I did so, I knew that the grace effectively imparted in the sacrament would have been mine in any case had I remained in my seat and silently invited the Lord to touch and fill me afresh just then and there that hot, sunny Easter morning.

1997: Twenty years later our grand adventure with the Lord in the Army found us in the United States. We had been sent to Massachusetts to take responsibility for the Army's work in that beautiful New England state. We loved it. We encountered American warmth and openness and a disarming readiness to talk naturally about the things of the spiritual life. I valued too my regular contacts with the other denominational leaders in the state. It was vitally important to let them know and feel that the Army saw itself as a church and not just as a social work agency.

The 1997 Annual General Meeting (AGM) of the Massachusetts Council of Churches was held at the Newton Andover Theological College. I ensured that our official delegation turned out in numbers. The AGM was preceded by a joint service in the College Chapel, which was planned in such a way that the sacrament of the Lord's Supper was its climax.

This was not Kariba. I was not on vacation, and I was not in my T–shirt and shorts! Because this was an official ecumenical event we felt that our best response was to remain in our seats during the sacrament, maintaining an attitude of prayer. We were, of course, very visible in our uniforms. It was important to be there, to be in solidarity with the believers from all the many other church traditions, but it was also important to witness quietly to the authenticity of Salvationist sacramentalism.

We stayed in our seats. So too did all the Roman Catholics, the Greek Orthodox priest (who had been specially invited as a step toward that church's formal membership in the Massachusetts Council of Churches), and so too did the sole Quaker representative. Everyone had gone to much trouble to be present that evening. We were all people of goodwill, with a spirit of mutual acceptance, and our Council of Churches coordinator had worked with sensitivity and skill to draw us all closer together over time. But making the Eucharist the centerpiece of the occasion left no fewer than four denominations very visibly on the sidelines. An occasion of unity became an occasion of visible disunity. With a deeper, subtler understanding of sacramentalism free from ritual, it need not have been so.

Chapter 4
Salvationist Sacramentalism

A Look Back • Precious Freedoms • Meanings and Definitions • Am I a Sacrament?

On reading the title to this chapter some will frown with puzzlement. "But I thought the Army did not have sacraments!" they will say. In a narrow sense this is true. Others will ask, "Aren't we supposed to be non–sacramental?" Again, in a strictly limited sense this is also true. So an explanation is due.

In this chapter I will try to explain that Salvationists have not always been careful in the vocabulary they use on this subject. Neither have we always realized the subtlety of what our writers and thinkers have been expressing. It is this writer's view that the Army has from its earliest days held within its collective subconscious a deep and meaningful understanding of sacramentalism, so that it is not entirely satisfactory to say we are "*non*–sacramental" or that we are "*not* sacramentalists."

The one clear thing that can be said right at the beginning is that The Salvation Army does not practice sacramental rituals. This statement does not automatically lead to the conclusion that Salvationists therefore cannot possibly be sacramentalists. I am advocating an understanding of sacramentalism that does not hinge upon any outward form or ceremony.

A Look Back

Army literature on the sacraments is not extensive. To read it all in a leisurely fashion would not take more than a day or two. *The War Cry* of January 17, 1883 carried an article in which William Booth addressed his officers. He wanted to be clear with them that "no sacrament can rightly be seen as a condition of salvation." He wanted the Army to be free from "the grave dissensions" that sometimes were associated with the sacraments.[1] A year earlier, in the November 4, 1882 *War Cry*, he had urged his officers never to speak against the sacraments, never to attempt to satirize them, but also to avoid taking Salvationists to church services if the sacrament were to be held there, and to leave churches if the sermon was on the subject of the sacraments.[2]

Now all this could easily be taken as an "anti–sacraments" stance. Not so. Before The Salvation Army took its name, it was The Christian Mission (1865–1878), and the Lord's Supper was a regular part of its worship. Many women and men came to Booth wanting to be identified with his work and mission. Catherine Booth was an immense influence upon her husband's thinking, and she believed in the spiritual validity of ministry by women. The crisis came when two principles clashed: the equality of women in all aspects of ministry, and the view held by some that only a man could authentically administer the sacrament of the Lord's Supper. These two could not coexist. After much heart searching and prayer, much discussion and agonizing, Booth came to the conclusion that nothing in Scripture compelled the view that any sacrament was essential to the salvation of a human soul. On that basis then the observance of sacraments ended, and the principle of equality for women in each and every aspect of Christian spiritual and practical ministry won the day.

Thus it was that The Salvation Army came no longer to hold sacramental rituals. However, the underlying concept of sacramentalism was not thereby abandoned. It is this that needs to be restated and reappreciated as we move into the twenty–first century.

Minnie Lindsay Carpenter, wife of General George Carpenter, wrote a booklet entitled *Salvationists and the Sacraments*. In it she describes the transition of the Army from mission to church: "The Salvation Army became definitely, and with every sign of permanence, a branch of the Christian church."[3] Then she mentions the influence of the Society of Friends (the Quakers) upon the Booths and other early Salvationists. She sees this influence as the explanation for the Army's belief that the deep, inner experience of grace could be, and was, real without any external rituals. William Booth, she wrote, "pointed his people to the privilege and necessity of seeking the substance rather than the shadow."[4]

It is here that we begin to sense the nature of Salvationist sacramentalism. In place of infant baptism, Booth introduced the dedicating of infants to God. In place of adult baptism, he used soldiership as his concept for membership of the church, and held a simple, but dignified, ceremony of swearing–in. The vital thing to grasp about these practices is that neither was seen as a sacrament in the traditional sense, yet they came rapidly to be regarded as a means of grace. In place of the Lord's Supper, he called upon his soldiers to let their daily lives be a continual recognition of their union with Christ, and to let every meal be a remembrance of Christ's dying. It is in these concepts that the seeds of Salvationist sacramentalism can be found. It is a sacramentalism free from ritual, independent of formal outward observances and material elements.

As part of the Army's Missionary Literature Series, a short book by William Metcalf entitled *The Salvationist and the Sacraments* was published in 1965. It is a thoughtful, scholarly work, written in unpretentious style with a beautiful simplicity of language. Metcalf writes: "God is equally pleased to meet us outside the sacraments or any other ceremony." He then offers the reader three distinct warnings. First, a warning about the danger of having *any* ceremony "which we repeat over and over again because we worship God in it," because we think God chooses to be uniquely present in the ceremony and only in the ceremony (this is the sense in which the word "ritual" is used in this chapter).[5] Second, he warns about the risk of forgetting that The Salvation Army is part of the prophetic tradition, which from Old Testament times has declared against all comers that ceremonial religion is not the only, or even the best, way to God. Third, Metcalf warns us about the risk of losing our corporate composure, our poise, our nerve when discovering the loneliness that obedience to God in our prophetic role can bring. Each of these three warnings has a clear contemporary relevance for The Salvation Army and for our sanctified self–assurance under God in the next century.

Clifford Kew's *Closer Communion* came out in 1980.[6] It sought to be somewhat more analytical than anything already published by the Army on the sacraments. Kew rightly stressed that our position did not originate in any ingrained prejudice against the sacraments, nor indeed from a desire just to be different, for it is at times a costly stance to uphold. Rather, it emerged on the anvil of pragmatic ecclesiological factors and as a result of steadily growing theological convictions. Here Kew is referring to what I call "God's ways and dealings with us." It is in these that we have our identity.

There are other dealings of God with the Army down through the years that have shaped and molded us. None should be lightly discarded. Each plays its part in making us who we are as a distinct people of God, and yet in His eternal and divine graciousness God has bestowed these distinctives in a way that none of them becomes a straightjacket. We are still gloriously free to adapt to changing times in our methods and in our responses to changing human needs. This keeps us relevant, but when the methods change, the message does not—and neither need the historically validated identity of the messenger. Part of that identity is our God–given insight into sacramentalism and the relationship of outward ritual to the receiving of divine grace.

More recently Commissioner Paul Rader, before being elected the General and international leader of The Salvation Army in 1994, was speaking to Hispanic Salvationists in the Western Territory of the United States.[7] It was May 9, 1994, and his topic was the sacraments. Many of his hearers would have come originally from a Roman Catholic culture in which the formalities of sacramental worship were seen as essential to a state of grace. Rader spoke to them of the strangely ambivalent role of the sacraments in church history. He openly acknowledged their validity for true and sincere believers as a means of grace, and yet they had also been "a cause for confusion and often bitter contention." He articulated the burning question facing not only The Salvation Army but the whole church: "Is God interested primarily in form or in function?"

Then he spelled out, with careful clarity, the Army's belief about the immediacy of grace:

> *We believe that the grace of Christ comes to us, not through the act of partaking of small pieces of bread or drinking small cups of grape juice or wine several times a year as it is given to us by certain accredited ministers of the Gospel empowered to do so. We believe the saving, sanctifying, purifying and empowering grace of Christ is available to us here and now as we reach out in faith to Him. We believe that this grace is made real in our hearts by the presence and the power of the Holy Spirit through faith. We would rather not join certain other churches in squabbling over who can take the communion and who can give it, how often it can be offered and how often it should be taken, whether it should be bread or crackers, wine or juice, taken in the seats or at the altar rail and the like. Our concern is whether or not we know personal communion with the Lord, whether we have come to Him and put our trust in Him. Jesus declared: "I am the bread of life. He who comes to me will never go hungry, and he who believes in me will never be thirsty."*[8]

Then came the single most important sentence in his presentation: "When our hearts are made holy, all of life is a sacrament."[9] Here then is Salvationist sacramentalism in a nutshell. It is closely interwoven with our understanding of mature spirituality, the sanctified life in the secular world and the blessing of a clean heart. The tenth of our Articles of Faith has already been quoted.[10] Arising directly out of this tenet is the belief that no part of our personalities is beyond the purifying touch of God, the Holy Spirit; that each and every aspect of our being can be held and kept free from sin by the power of God if yielded in full obedience to His will and purposes; that God will work through such a life to impart grace to others, making of that life a sacrament; and that grace will be imparted to that life by all or any means chosen by God since the whole of the created order is sacred to the sanctified believer, making redundant the need to single out some particular element as a uniquely special agent of grace. Neither God nor His grace can be thus confined.

Finally, Rader reminded his hearers of their right to witness to the reality of divine grace imparted to the soul without ritual or ceremony, a truth that places enormous responsibility upon the believer who so claims. It is vital to the interests of the church as a whole that Salvationists maintain and articulate this witness, for many in the traditional sacramental denominations have expressed appreciation for the Army's counterbalancing emphasis upon the reality and authenticity of divine grace received without reliance upon outward form.

Precious Freedoms

The view that Salvationism is truly and deeply sacramentalist will surprise not only some of our Christian friends in other churches, but will find its critics within the Army. These latter will fall largely into two camps. One camp will say that we are a sacrament–free zone, and there is no need to muddy the waters by speaking of sacramentalism without ritual. The other will say that it makes no sense to claim we are sacramentalists without adopting the accompanying ceremonies of the other churches. Both criticisms stem from a failure to distinguish between "sacrament" and "ritual." My claim is that it can indeed make theological sense to speak of a sacramental life even though the believer has never partaken of a sacramental ceremony of any kind. Conversely, it is possible to participate in sacramental ceremonies on a regular basis and yet not be living a sacramental life. The authenticity of a sacramental life is not dependent upon ceremony at all. It is a life of freedom. It is free from the constraints of outward forms, free from the controversies surrounding the diversity of sacramental and ritualistic dogma and free from the sense of separation that haunts so many Christians who cannot or will not share their rituals with those seen as outsiders.

Gladly today almost all churches, with the notable exception of the Roman Catholic church (in October 1998 the catholic Bishops of Britain and Ireland published a positional statement, *One Bread, One Body*, which again refused to open the Roman sacrament to non–Catholic believers), will receive at the communion rail any full member of another church. The recent call by the Archbishop of Canterbury, Dr. George Carey, for the Catholics to look seriously at shared Eucharistic practice is timely. The twenty–first century needs an essentially undivided body of Christ. Salvationists feel no need to take a view one way or another of the theologies of other churches in relation to their sacraments or outward forms. Salvationist sacramentalism leaves the Salvationist free to relate even–handedly to all other denominations and traditions. Each practice is respected; none is criticized. All who find them spiritually helpful will receive encouragement from the Army to continue to use them. However, the Salvationist is called by God to demonstrate the practical feasibility of living daily and hourly a pure and Christlike life by grace through faith in Jesus, without the help of sacramental ritual. Many of us experience this as a harder, but higher, way.

This is Salvationist sacramentalism. It is not a difficult thing to grasp. It has no complex theology. It is, however, almost unheard of outside The Salvation Army and the Society of Friends. There is a precious, golden thread running through Army literary sources on this subject that has not always been made explicit. It emerges from all the writers quoted above in a combination of the following shared emphases:

• Sacramental ceremonies or rituals are not to be scorned.

- No ceremony is essential to salvation, including the sacrament of the Lord's Supper and baptism.

- No ceremony is essential to a life lived in obedience to the commands of Christ or to growing in grace.

- Though we may regard the rituals as dispensable, the grace sought therein is not.

- The Army is called to witness to all this, reminding the whole church concerning the immediacy and direct accessibility of grace quite apart from any outward form.

- This witness will be misunderstood by many. It will mean loneliness often. Some will say, because of it, that we are not a church.

- Our doctrine of the holy life is inextricably interwoven with all of this. That life is itself a sacrament, being used of God to channel real grace to others.

Meanings and Definitions

This last point reminds us that according to the *Book of Common Prayer* a sacrament is "an outward and visible sign of an inward and spiritual grace."[11] Salvationist sacramentalism carries this to its logical conclusion and says that a person can be such a sign, derivatively from Christ, the one True Sacrament. You can be a sacrament. I can be a sacrament.

The 1994 *Catechism of the Catholic Church* says that sacraments are "powers that come forth from the Body of Christ" (a definition from the 1547 Council of Trent).[12] They are "actions of the Holy Spirit at work in His Body, the Church," they are "the masterworks of God in the new covenant."[13] The *Catechism* does not admit the possibility of the Christlike life of an ordinary believer being within any of these definitions, for within Catholicism a sacrament is thought of in the narrow terms of a ceremony. At best a Christlike life would be seen as a "sacramental," a mere reminder of the grace or presence of God. It is the Army's belief that such a life actually imparts and channels grace to others since, by the Holy Spirit, the real presence of Christ indwells the believer.

The medieval church had no fewer than twelve sacraments. Today the Catholic church has seven: baptism, confirmation, Eucharist, penance, anointing the sick, holy orders, and matrimony.[14] All are seen as having been personally instituted by Christ. Protestants usually recognize only two sacraments: baptism and the Lord's Supper. The other five are not regarded as "sacraments of the Gospels." So from the outset we are thrown up against a difference of belief, and even before we can ask what meaning each church attaches to each sacrament, we are forcibly drawn into argument about how many sacraments there are. According to Salvationist sacramentalism the number of possible sacraments is infinite, for the potential number of Christlike believers is infinite.

An examination of official Catholic teaching about the fruits of Holy Communion is revealing. The 1994 *Catechism* lists six fruits:

- Intimate union with Christ
- Separation from sin
- Preservation from future mortal sin
- Consolidation of the Church
- Commitment of the believer to the poor
- Inspiration to work for the unity of all believers.[15]

It is a fascinating list. A Salvationist response might be as follows:

•Intimate union with Christ is offered in the Gospel of John repeatedly without reference to ceremony: Jesus is the believer's Light, the believer's Shepherd, the believer's Living Water, the believer's Living Bread, the believer's Door to the place of salvation and safety. He is our Way, our Truth, our Life. He is our True Vine.

Salvationist hymns are ripe with doctrinal content on the practical possibility of a life separated from sin, a holy life.

- We believe passionately in, and experience daily, the possibility of ongoing victory over temptation.

- Our ninth and tenth Doctrines teach about the grace that holds us in our new–found salvation and which can preserve us faultless until the coming of our Lord Jesus Christ.[16]

- We know and experience that mystical union with believers in any denomination who confess Jesus as Lord, not feeling that we need to limit our concept of the church to one denomination regardless of its age, size or influence.

- The Army is committed to the poor, placing high priority on self–denying advocacy and service.

- We also pray and work actively across every continent of the earth for the unity of all believers. Yet we have no sacramental ceremonies. Grace is not subject to ceremony. It is appropriated by faith.

Am I a Sacrament?

Are *you* a sacrament? Am *I* a sacrament? Put like this, the question will either offend or bring deep personal challenge. Yet in terms of Salvationist sacramentalism it makes total sense. The following poem by Albert Orsborn, former General of The Salvation Army, cannot be properly understood unless the simple but profound notion of Salvationist sacramentalism is also understood:

> *My life must be Christ's broken bread,*
> *My love His outpoured wine,*

A cup o'erfilled, a table spread
Beneath His name and sign,
That other souls, refreshed and fed,
May share His life through mine.
My all is in the Master's hands
For Him to bless and break;
Beyond the brook His winepress stands
And thence my way I take,
Resolved the whole of love's demands
To give, for His dear sake.

Lord, let me share that grace of Thine
Wherewith Thou didst sustain
The burden of the fruitful vine,
The gift of buried grain.
Who dies with Thee, O Word divine,
Shall rise and live again.

(Albert Orsborn)[17]

Orsborn has bequeathed to the whole church, not only to Salvationists, an eloquent manifesto of the possibility of the believer's life and love becoming a sacrament by which others are fed in their souls and built up in their faith. Each of us can give the Lord Jesus Christ our lives and our love. No outward ceremony is needed, no special place, no special time. Right where you are now will do. He can and will take our unworthy lives, our imperfect love, and graciously use them to nourish others.

Perhaps it is fitting that the final word in this chapter should be given to a Roman Catholic disciple of Christ, the American monk, Thomas Merton. It is a short extract from his writings quoted by M. Basil Pennington. In it Merton offers an almost Salvationist understanding of a sacrament, seeing our daily life and routine as a channel of grace:

The best thing that goes on is nothing. It is the
spaces, when we simply are to God and He is to
us. It is the daily routine which becomes a trans

parent sacrament of God's presence and the conatural vehicle of our being present to Him. This is what is important. It is the context for everything else.[18]

Chapter 5
Should the Army Change?

Defining the Question • Pressure for Change • The Case for Change • An Unproven Case • What Would Change Mean in Practice? • Diagnosis or Misdiagnosis?

Defining the Question

Should the Army change its position on the sacraments? This is a question raised from time to time, and in the last few years it has been pressed more and more in some parts of the Army world. There is a need to be sure just what the question means. The previous chapter was an attempt to articulate in a positive and constructive way Salvationist sacramentalism. For too long the Army has responded defensively to inquirers or critics on the matter of sacraments. We have a holy tradition and a sacred history that has led us to our present attitude under the guidance of God, the Holy Spirit. We can, therefore, be confidently relaxed about it. There is no need to be defensive or to feel that somehow we are second-rate believers because we do not include sacramental ritual in our worship events. We have been called as a people to a distinctive and, in many senses, harder way. Some among us would wish also to see it as a higher way, for it looks beyond the confines of material elements and outward forms, opening up new vistas for freedom in Christ.

What does it mean when change is asked for? Most who ask for it do not mean that they want us to abandon what in the last chapter I call "Salvationist sacramentalism," for they would not be likely to have understood this to be part of the Army's tradition. What they are asking for is the introduction (or to be more historically precise, the reintroduction) of sacramental ritual. They see an easier path. They believe they are asking for the Army to become *sacramentalist*, but we have always been that, for the reasons already spelled out. The grounds for seeking to reintroduce sacramental ritual (as distinct from sacramentalism itself) are not always clear. We need to look carefully and objectively at the case for change.

Pressure for Change

The disquiet in some places about sacramental ritual is not new. As a young Salvationist, and long before I was an officer, I heard the view expressed that we ought to have a ceremony like the other "proper churches." Young as I was, this struck me as odd. I intuited a sense of inferiority in some of my older fellow Salvationists. As a captain working at International Headquarters in the mid 1980s, I recall clearly a lunchtime conversation with no less than three English lieutenant colonels, all of whom told me solemnly and in absolute seriousness that unless the Army went back to sacramental ritual it would sound our death knell! I could hardly believe my ears, and I lost my appetite for lunch!

Often the amount of pressure for change is overstated. Voices raised in dissent tend to be louder than the moderate majority. It is certainly true that some, not all, of our leaders in Roman Catholic cultures, where our numbers have never been large, think that having ritual in our worship will encourage new converts to stay with us for they will then see us as a "proper church." In other parts of the Army world there are a few, here and there, who advocate change, often with real passion and conviction. Their reasons vary from person to person. Some think we are being disobedient to a clear command of Christ. Some think the Army has lost its spiritual and evangelical cutting–edge and a sacramental ritual will remedy this. Some think that our worship has grown stale and arid and that a sacramental ritual will revive it. Some think that we are so out on a limb compared with the other churches that we should reintroduce sacramental ritual so as to be truly accepted at the ecumenical table. Do these proffered grounds for change betray perhaps a failure to grasp the true and deep meaning of Salvationist sacramentalism? Could it be that, theologically speaking, we are being asked to step down, not up?

Some seeking change, however, express a real and genuine sense of distress. They see some of our halls and sanctuaries unfilled and wonder if a new ritual would fill them. Some of our young people are told by non–Salvationists that if they are not baptized in water, they cannot possibly be saved. This is terribly distressing. Some see the number of cadets entering our officer training colleges in sharp decline in some countries and wonder if a new ceremony will increase the numbers. They look also at the drop in formal memberships, especially in Europe, and again speculate about the cause. Can it be our lack of sacramental ritual?

I suspect that these negative patterns result from a complex combination of social and cultural factors, for they are not found everywhere. They have to do also with the life cycle of organizations and the necessity of revisioning by each generation, for these patterns are more often found where the Army is older, not where it is still comparatively young. It is in fact very difficult to see a clear logical connection between any of these trends and the issue of whether or not The Salvation Army should abandon Salvationist sacramentalism and instead start holding a new ritual in its meetings and worship events. What is more likely is that advocates for change, not having a full appreciation of Salvationist sacramentalism, or of its depths, or of its implications for them personally, start from the initial premise that the Army should have sacramental ceremonies and then attribute all our problems and all our malaises to their absence. Yet no causal link has ever been established.

Any case for the reintroduction of sacramental ritual has to be thought through with the strongest intellectual rigor. There are many questions to answer. Some of these are theological, some ecclesiological and others plain pragmatic.

The Case for Change

The most articulate case for change that I have come across recently was that made by a member of the Army's International Spiritual Life Commission at the Commission's April 1997 meeting in London, England. It was a minority view among the members of the Commission, but is deserving of much respect and of repetition here. It consists of ten thoughtful points, which I will try to restate faithfully:

- The reintroduction of sacramental ritual would settle the issue of whether or not the Army is being disobedient to a direct command of the Lord recorded in New Testament Scripture.

- It would be faithful to our historical roots and to who we once were up to 1882 when the decision was taken no longer to hold sacramental rituals.

- William Booth deliberately left the issue open for future generations to decide if need be.

- The present Salvationist position carries within it a danger of rejecting any link between matters of the soul and the physical world, something that in the days of the early Church led to the heresy of Gnosticism (the belief that the creator is evil, that the world is an evil and alien place, that salvation is based upon the obtaining of secret spiritual knowledge, is for the soul alone and is not for the body).

- It is inherent in the traditions of Protestantism to reform and to reconfess the faith in each generation, unlike the Roman Catholic view that the corpus of the faith is handed down once and for all as a *depositum fide*, and so the Army is free in this or in any generation to opt for significant doctrinal change.

• If in our earliest days we were but a sect or a mission, that is no longer the case for today; we are a church, and having sacramental ritual would therefore be appropriate.

• The Army is called by God to use whatever means will win the lost; why not use sacramental ritual?

• In the post–modern world, Christianity will become more and more marginalized so that the churches will need one another more than ever, and having a sacramental ritual will assist the Army to be closer to the mainstream churches.

• The sacrament of the Lord's Supper has been shown by reason, by experience and by tradition to be helpful in the lives of countless believers.

• It is in the Army's best traditions to be adaptable, and so we could use sacramental ritual where it is wanted or needed, but not where those reasons do not apply, each territory choosing its own doctrinal position and practice.[1]

An Unproven Case

Let us consider each of these ten points in turn:

• This is the most powerful of the points given. In Luke 22:19, and in the synoptic parallel verses, we find the words of Jesus as He takes bread and wine and says, "Do this in remembrance of me." These words have come to be known as the "words of institution," that is to say they are taken by most believers as words spoken by Jesus to establish a perpetual ceremony. This is, of course, not their only interpretation. Everything hinges on the meaning of the word "this." Do "this." Do what? What were they all doing in the upper room when Jesus said, "Do this"?

The simple and obvious answer is that they were celebrating the Jewish Passover. Jesus was telling His disciples, all of whom were Jewish, that in future when they celebrated the Passover they should do so in remembrance of Him and not of Moses. For people who have never celebrated the Passover and are never likely to, the words, "Do this," may therefore be taken not to apply. This point of view will, I know, be dismissed immediately by any reader who has a background in a church with sacramental ritual at its heart. It is exceedingly difficult to throw off centuries of conditioning and suddenly to see words that we revere given a whole new meaning.

A different interpretation does not entail any lesser degree of reverence for anything and everything spoken by Jesus, but both spiritual and intellectual courage is needed to get beyond the automatic assumption that these words are in fact "words of institution." It has not and cannot be shown beyond reasonable doubt that when Jesus said, "Do this," he was intending to institute anything at all.

• It is true that from 1865–1882 the Lord's Supper was used in The Christian Mission and in the Army (the name "The Salvation Army" was used for the first time in 1878). However, the path of God's dealings with us then began to take shape, and the emergence of Salvationist sacramentalism represents an integral part of our emerging identity as the Army and the sort of church we are today. Who we were in the days before The Salvation Army was called by that name, and in the four short years after 1878, is a precious part of our very early history, but cannot be treated as determinative of who we should be in the twenty-first century. A few short years of continuing ritual practice brought in from other church traditions ought not to be seen as overriding the long years of God's ways with us since that time to the present day.

- William Booth was a man who knew exactly when to be dogmatic and when to be flexible. The historical evidence after 1883 for Booth actually believing that later generations of Salvationists would reverse the position he came to under the guidance of the Holy Spirit is at best meager. A little internal politics must inevitably have been in play when the debate was current in The Christian Mission. The pressure on Booth from all sides and all opinions would have been very strong indeed. He wanted unanimity, but if he could not get it he would settle for nothing less than solidarity. Why risk schism? The waverers would have to be content with a passing hint that the matter might at some unspecified future date be reopened.[2] Booth was many things, including an astute pragmatist. It is my belief that his fleeting mention of some possible future revisiting of the issue was designed for those of his contemporaries who were unsure of their position and was never intended seriously as a mandate for future change. This is supported by the fact that from Booth down to the establishment of the Interna-

tional Spiritual Life Commission in 1996, none
of the Army's international leaders has ever seriously contemplated such a step. If change is to
happen, it needs to be predicated upon much
firmer ground than a short and solitary sentence
in a single article written 115 years ago.

- The fear of the Army lapsing somehow into the
classical heresy of Gnosticism is a subtle academic
argument, but is entirely overstated. Salvationists are far too down to earth, far too practiced in
the appreciation of the created order to fall into
any belief that matter (everything we can appreciate with our physical senses) is bad. We shall
still be singing, well into the twenty–first century,
"O Lord my God, when I in awesome wonder,
consider all the works Thy hands have made ...
How great Thou art!"[3] We shall never believe that
the Creator is evil or that the salvation offered us
in Christ is not for the body but only for the soul.
To suggest that we might is to fail to grasp the
centrality of our holiness teaching, which explicitly states that our whole spirit, soul and body
will be kept blameless until Jesus comes again.
The argument based on the risk of the Army being overtaken by Gnosticism need not detain us
longer here.

- It is true that in the traditions of the Reformation
we accept that each new generation is free to re-
interpret and to re–express the faith for its own
contemporary setting. Salvationists do have room
for this as each era comes and goes, and the suc-
cessive editions of our *Handbook of Doctrine*, along
with other Army literature, bear witness to this.
However, this freedom does not give license to

cast away lightly the ways and dealings of God with us through the years. Neither does it invite us suddenly to change who we are under God. We are a people to whom God has granted many distinctives as He has graciously shaped and molded us. Salvationists can and will disagree about what these are. It raises the question of what is and is not negotiable.

It is the view of this writer that our distinctive concept of Salvationist sacramentalism is from God and ought not to be discarded. It is given to us to be received, to be embraced, to be thought through, to be taught, to be lived out and to be applied. It has not been given to us to throw away. Also, I wonder whether the advocates of change are open to the possibility of first reintroducing sacramental ritual and then having a later generation drop it again! It would be an odd way of doing theology, and a strange way of being a church to be taken seriously.

• It is at best dubious to suggest that now the Army is a "proper church," we need sacramental ritual to be convincing. This stems from a false assumption that respectability in ecclesiastical circles depends upon having particular forms in your worship events. If we are not a proper church now, changing to sacramental ritual will not alter things. Even if we were to reintroduce a ceremony, say the Lord's Supper, there would still be many who would regard what we were doing as "not the real thing" compared with their ceremony! It is precisely this theological squabbling from which the good Lord in His infinite wisdom has set us free! Why go downwards and backwards into controversy, with all its debilitating drain upon our energies and time? Let us be confident in who and what we are. In chapter 1 the entire question of whether the Army is a church was opened up and answered with a resounding "Yes!" It is neither wise nor dignified to dig away at the foundations of our identity as a distinctive church merely to appease the doubters. We do not see the Old Testament prophets backtracking on who and what God wanted them to be just because some doubted their authenticity. Nor do we see Jesus being swayed by those who thought He was not a proper Messiah!

• The Army has shown again and again its readiness to use all and any means to spread the gospel. The idea of reintroducing sacramental ritual in order to do so is to fail to understand the purpose and meaning of that ritual. It is not a ceremony for unbelievers, but for believers. Neither is there any hard evidence that our non–use of such ritual is keeping anyone outside the Kingdom of God. Moreover, the argument fails to see that our position on Salvationist sacramentalism is not just a matter of what we do but is part of who we are, and this cannot be discarded for purposes of temporary expediency.

• It is a pessimistic view to assume that the fate of Christianity in the twenty–first century will be one of inexorable decline and marginalization. Christians in the west may feel this is not unlikely, but if you take a global and international view it will be seen that the church is growing—and growing rapidly—in many parts of the world once deemed "missionary" lands. This is certainly true of the worldwide Army. For example, here in

Pakistan the Army's adult memberships are growing at a current rate of about 10 percent per an-
num, and the number of persons in full–time
ministry as officers is rising at an even faster rate,
so much so that we have difficulty sometimes in
seeing how we can afford to fund and deploy all
who would embark upon this vocation (as I write
we have 80 excellent applications for the 30 places
in our training college).[4] It is a good problem to
have! Why then should we assume that the future is bleak? Why should we think that God is
not a God of victory who can and will revive His
church and once more use His people influen-
tially in any walk of life?

Marginalization is not our inescapable destiny, nor is it the will of God for Christ's body on
earth. Even supposing it were, how would having sacramental ritual draw us closer to the traditional churches? Whatever ritual we introduced
might draw us closer to one, but drive us further
away from the others! Furthermore, we have a
duty under God to witness to the practical possibility of a sacramental life free from ritual, and
this duty remains whether the church as a whole
is going through good times or bad. It is not hard
to find thoughtful friends in other churches who
cherish their sacramental practices, and yet who
will say openly and warmly that they are glad and
grateful for the witness of the Army in this aspect
of the Christian life. We ought to think hard before we let these people down.

• The helpfulness and value of the Lord's Supper,
and indeed of other sacramental outward forms,
has never been in doubt. Many testify to this, and
the Army has never denied it. In itself this is no

reason to abandon Salvationist sacramentalism. Our calling is to demonstrate that the help and nourishment others derive from the sacrament is ours directly and immediately by faith. To change would be to deny that this is so. The potential loneliness of our position has been recognized from the beginning. We are not to expect anything different. But the fact that obedience to the Lord's will is costly has never been a reason for turning back. It is better to please God than to join the crowd, even if that crowd is ever so respectable from an ecclesiastical point of view! Endurance and courage in the face of misunderstanding are gifts that God has frequently bestowed upon His Army. He is a God who specializes in helping His people keep their nerve.

• The notion of having some sort of sacramental ritual in some Army territories and not in others is a recipe for chaos! Our historical position on Salvationist sacramentalism is a matter of doctrine, even though it is not enshrined in our formal Articles of Faith. A mark of a true church is that its doctrine is adhered to throughout its ranks. Where else in the world could we find a church that encourages, even plans for, such fundamental divergence of doctrinal belief and practice from culture to culture, country to country? Expressions of the gospel may vary, but the basic doctrines do not. Presentation may be diverse, but not the substance.

What Would Change Mean in Practice?

It is not clear that the practical, grassroots implications of reintroducing sacramental ritual to The Salvation Army have been completely understood by those anxious to see change. I cannot, of course, claim to have heard or spoken to all who want to go back to the pre–1882 position, but I have had the benefit of serving on four continents, have travelled for 20 years to almost every part of the Army world and have mixed and conversed, during 13 years, with over 60 sessions of officer delegates from every corner of the globe as they have attended the International College for Officers in London, England. Naturally, one listens with special care when the topic of the sacraments crops up. I have to confess that in all of this I have not yet heard an exhaustive treatment of the pragmatic consequences of change. An appeal to the emotions has its place, but with it must come clear evidence that all the many practical complexities of abandoning Salvationist sacramentalism have been addressed and dealt with. To these we turn now.

Any serious proposal for change must spell out the reasons for a sudden U–turn in our doctrinal position. It must convince the worldwide Army that we have been wrong about God's ways and dealings with us, or at least that He has now chosen to discharge us from what has previously been a calling to witness to the rest of His body on earth and to the wider world. A proposal for change needs also to explain why it is that the church as a whole has moved beyond any need for such a counter–balancing witness, for no other group is out there ready to assume our mantle.

Advocates for change must tell us what they think a sacrament is, with equally clear teaching on what they think a sacrament is not. What shall we teach our people on the meaning of a sacrament? Which of all the prevailing theologies shall we adopt? With which sacramental school of thought shall we take sides? Why one and not another? The call for change involves an entirely novel teaching for the Army.

A proposal for change must also tell us how many sacraments we shall observe ritually, with the reasons spelled out why some now observed in other churches might not be adopted in our ranks. Will we observe seven? If not, why not? Shall we keep to the dominical rituals, that is, those that are claimed to have been instituted by Jesus: baptism and the Lord's Supper? If only these, why only these, when for generations we have said to the world that the evidence to support Christly institution is at best slim?

Pro–change Salvationists also need to tell us what form the new rituals will take. For baptism, will we immerse or sprinkle? Will we do for infants whatever it is that we will do for adults? Are we ready to get embroiled in the infant baptism controversy? Where will our baptisms be held—indoors or outdoors? Shall we use still water or flowing water, or does it not matter? If it does not matter, why does it not matter, when to other believers it seems to matter a great deal? How will we interpret the New Testament practices, and how closely will we try to follow them?

What format and what elements shall we use for the Lord's Supper? Shall we in fact use that name for it? Even the very choice of what we call it will paint us into one ritualistic corner or another. Will it be like a Passover meal, thus ensuring that at least in its form we are as close as possible to what was done at the Last Supper? What will the Army ritual take in from the Catholic Eucharist, from the Anglican communion ceremony, from the Lutheran tradition or from a Free Church remembrance occasion?

What theology shall we attach to the new things we shall be doing in our worship? What can we tell the world's Salvationists is the theological and spiritual significance of it all? What are we to tell them is happening in the ritual that did not and could not happen, and which was not available to us by faith, before we embraced the ritual?

If reintroduction of these things is designed to cure the Army of its ills (we acknowledge that we have some), how shall we measure worldwide whether or not the new rituals are curing these ills? How will we know? When will we know? Can we even agree initially about what these ills actually are, for this is necessary before we can see if they have been remedied? If the new rituals fail to cure, will we readopt our prophetic stance and witness based on classical Salvationist sacramentalism or will it somehow be too late by then?

How often are we to hold the new practices? Some suggest monthly or even once a quarter and have written to Salvationist periodicals to say so. Why at these intervals? No explanations are offered. It is all done by "feel." If these rituals are important enough to run the risk of the entire Salvation Army turning away from its divinely historical calling under God in this matter, how can they be so unimportant as to be relegated to a mere "now and again" observance? Weekly must surely be the sensible arrangement, thus changing irreversibly the character and thrust of our worship where the focal point today is not a ritual but the Scriptures, the Word of God, preached and proclaimed. Even our architecture and the internal design of our halls and meeting rooms is determined so as to reflect the centrality of the Scriptures and their expounding. Now the rituals will be central. I say this because how can anything less than absolutely central be put forward as sufficient ground for a claim that God has changed his mind about the Army, and that what has been seen for so long as part of our birthright may now be cast aside.

Any proposal for change that is comprehensive must also tell us what place the new rituals will have in our key worship events apart from regular Sunday worship services. Will we be having divisional sacramental rituals? Will we be seeing territorial rituals at commissionings, public welcome meetings, and the like? If not, why not? Will these rituals be used in our training colleges, in our officers' councils, in our local officers' seminars, at our youth councils? If so, what shall we tell those present we are doing now? What is it that will be happening in the new ceremony that could not or did not happen before? Will participation be mandatory for officers? Will, for example, a divisional commander be required by the Army's leaders to preside, to serve or otherwise to participate? If so, on what grounds?

This last question leads to another enormous and thorny issue. What provision will the Army make for those soldiers, local officers or officers whose consciences will not allow them to be a part of whatever it is that change and abandonment of Salvationist sacramentalism will bring? Do the advocates of change think that everyone will meekly fall into line? The onus is on them to spell out what plans they have for keeping the international Army intact, one coherent body in the face of such radical innovation. They must tell us what provision will be made to protect the consciences of those for whom being in the Army is due, at least in very significant part, to our historic, courageous, prophetic and often lonely stand on the relationship of ritual to the receiving of divine grace. Any serious proposal for change must convince us that these consciences will not be ridden–over roughshod and also demonstrate why these Salvationists would still be wanted as part of some new, history–free, but ritually–sensitive, Army! For many the whole matter goes very deep indeed. There are great risks for the integrity of the Army if this is underestimated. Schism is not God's will for us. Our international and cross–cultural identity is a sacred trust, and will become even more so as the world gets smaller and smaller in the information age of the twenty–first century.

What will happen should a divisional commander who welcomes such change says to his superiors, "Do not send me officers who do not favor the new practices"? What will happen when the local officers of a corps say to their divisional commander, "We do not want change here, but our corps officer does, so please remove him"? What will be the next step when an officer serving on the staff of a training college says, "My conscience will not let me teach these novel things to the cadets"? What will happen within candidates boards and councils when a candidate for officership says, "I am called to be an officer, but I cannot support the new rituals"? What will happen if a corps officer says, "I want only pro–change people on my corps council"? What will happen when a territorial commander tells International Headquarters that he wants around him in senior positions only those officers who share his sacramental outlook? What will happen when a leading officer, for the sake of conscience, will not participate in the new ritual on some important public occasion?

A proposal for change must also tell us what we are to say to the other churches about a sudden *volte face*. Many of them do in fact truly respect and understand our present position. Some have consistently pleaded with us not to change it, telling us with genuine Christian warmth and love that they welcome our witness as a corrective and a reminder of the risks of ritualism. In what terms shall we tell them they are now wrong? What line of reasoning shall we adopt to persuade them that we are still to be taken seriously? How shall we meet the gaze of those others who have never quite understood where we were coming from, but who now will see us, perhaps patronizingly, as seeking to ape our sacramental betters—and still not quite managing it?

Diagnosis or Misdiagnosis?

In this chapter I have referred to a view that the Army is suffering here and there from some sort of malaise. This is heard most often in western cultures, and not only in the Army, for many western churches are also experiencing changing times and diminishing memberships. Compared to some, the Army is not so badly off. It seems too facile a view to suggest that all will be right if only we can have sacramental ceremonies.

If there is indeed some measure of malaise, to what might it be due? At the risk of oversimplification I want to suggest one possible cause. The Army has been raised up by God to live, work and witness for His glory. We do this by obedience to Him. Obedience comes in discerning His will and purposes and aligning ourselves as a movement with them. For the whole of our history, we have been the recipients of a vocation under God to preach salvation from sin for the unregenerate person and sanctification of life for the saved person. Salvation and holiness are our twin banners. All our evangelical work and all our social work are carried out under the ethos of these twin doctrines. We still profess to believe in them both—salvation and holiness.

Could it be that these days we are doing better at the salvation part than at the holiness part? Is it just possible that we are beginning to lose our way in relation to the doctrine of the blessing of a clean heart? There are perhaps some visible signs. Some Army Trade departments no longer stock the works of Samuel Logan Brengle. Fewer officers preach fewer and fewer holiness sermons and hold fewer and fewer holiness Bible studies. The works of John Wesley are read hardly at all, and the works of Brengle can be heard spoken of in patronizing tones, as though he simply got it all wrong and today we are much more sophisticated! More and more of our

Brengle Institutes are becoming simply general retreats, with reading lists that do not include the classical holiness movement's seminal texts. Less and less we use holiness songs in our meetings, and less and less are they explained or understood. Could it be that we are letting slip, bit by bit, our holiness heritage? True, we still hold holiness meetings all over the world every Sunday morning, but you can attend for months and months and never hear a holiness sermon preached or a holiness testimony spoken.

I have generalized. In many places our holiness doctrine is well understood and keenly espoused by newcomers and long–serving Salvationists alike. This is especially true in North America. However, elsewhere there are signs of neglect. So when General Rader tells us that instead of worrying about sacraments we should concentrate upon living a life of holiness, he is getting it absolutely right.[5] It is not ritual that we lack, but holiness. Ritual will not cure us if the Army is ill, but full obedience to our first calling will always be a prerequisite of health as part of the body of Christ. It is not novelty that we need, but rediscovery of the things that once we knew, which once we believed and taught and to which we once testified. I ask not for a return to old methodologies, but for a contemporary, relevant, twenty–first century fidelity to the core values and truths that God long ago graciously entrusted to our stewardship.

Commissioner Brengle once wrote:

> *One of the Army's central doctrines and most valued and precious experiences is that of heart holiness. The bridge that the Army throws across the impassable gulf that separates the sinner from the Savior—who pardons that he might purify, who saves that he might sanctify—rests upon these two abutments—the forgiveness of sins through simple, penitent, obedient faith in a crucified Redeemer, and the purifying of the heart and empowering of the soul through the anointing of the Holy Spirit, given by its risen and anointed Lord, and re-*

*ceived not by works, but by faith. Remove ei-
ther of these abutments and the bridge falls;
preserve them in strength, and a world of lost
and despairing sinners can be confidently invited and urged to come and be gloriously
saved.*[6]

He also wrote:

*Without the doctrine (of holiness), the standard,
the teaching, we shall never find the experience
or, having found it we shall be likely to lose it.
Without the experience we shall neglect the
teaching, we shall doubt or despise the doctrine,
we shall lower the standard. When Officers lose
the experience, the Holiness Meetings languish,
and when they languish, the spiritual life of
the Corps droops and falls, and all manner of
substitutes and expedients are introduced to
cover up the ghastly facts of spiritual loss, dis-
ease and death.*[7]

Brengle's voice reaches us across the decades. In seeking to
evaluate the spiritual life of the Army as we enter the twenty–first
century, let us be sure that we are still obedient to our calling to
teach and live both salvation and holiness and that we are not
being inadvertently sidetracked, or subtly seduced, by "all manner
of substitutes and expedients."[8]

Chapter 6

The International Spiritual Life Commission

Members and Methods • Dr. John Austin Baker • The Commission's Report • God–Given Freedom • Baptism • The Lord's Supper • The Love Feast and Other Meals • Worship • Spiritual Disciplines • Teaching

---

Everything discussed in the last chapter has significant implications for the spirituality of Salvationists everywhere. As we move into the twenty–first century, the Army is going through a period of honest introspection and constructive self–examination of its own spiritual life. This is a very healthy thing to be doing, not least at a time when we are reaching a watershed transition from one century to another. News of the creation of the International Spiritual Life Commission (ISLC) by General Paul Rader in 1996 was widely greeted with warm gratitude, for Salvationists are activists first and foremost and easily vulnerable to spiritual burnout.[1] Many of us are in danger of neglecting our inner life under the harsh pressures of sheer busyness and the perceived need to succeed. Furthermore, some felt it was time to look again at our public worship life, including the question of our teaching on sacraments.

For these reasons the ISLC came into being with a mandate to examine every aspect of the spiritual life of the worldwide Army— a huge assignment!—and to work on a two year timetable so that the findings might be presented at the International Conference of Leaders in Melbourne, Australia in March 1998.

Members and Methods

A total of seventeen persons from all over the world, both officers and non–officers, became attending members of the Commission. Additional people, again from a wide variety of countries and cultures, were invited to serve on the Commission as corresponding members, and a few of these were able also to attend one or two meetings in person. The first chairman was Commissioner Ian Cutmore, then principal of the International College for Officers (ICO) in London. However, shortly after the work of the Commission began Commissioner Cutmore became the territorial commander in the New Zealand and Fiji territory and was succeeded by the Commission's Vice Chairman, Lt. Colonel Robert Street, training principal for the United Kingdom.

Five formal meetings of the attending members took place in London, England over a period of two years, each meeting lasting one week. The Commission's methodology was entirely flexible and allowed for the preparation and presentation of scholarly papers on key subjects, as well as more informal exchanging of views and ideas. Each special paper was subjected to close analysis and discussion. Free interaction by all the members, with growing mutual respect for differences of opinion, marked the sessions. Time was also carefully set aside for prayer together, and for shared worship. Written representations poured in, not only from officially appointed corresponding members, but from Salvationists everywhere who were anxious that no voice should go unheard. Every written submission was shared at the five meetings, with all the documentation being made available to each member.

General Paul Rader was kept closely informed of the progress of the work, and several times sat with the Commission for discussion and to offer ongoing encouragement. He stressed that the Army world needed to hear what the Commission felt led of the Holy Spirit to say and was very clear also that no aspect of our spiritual life and traditions need be treated as though exempt from scrutiny and re–evaluation.

A particular highlight of the process was a visit paid to the Commission on March 24, 1997 by a former Chairman of the

Church of England's Doctrine Commission, Bishop (Dr.) John Austin Baker. This was an encounter helpful in so many ways that it is worth relating here some of the views expressed by the Bishop.

Dr. John Austin Baker

Tall, lean and with a self–effacing air, the Bishop came into the lecture room at the ICO, venue for the Commission meeting in March 1997. He appeared relaxed and friendly, having something of a twinkle in his eye, but also the look of a perceptive leader of the people of God. Later, in his own hand, he wrote a letter of thanks to the Chairman to say that his day with the Commission members was "one of the most enjoyable days of Christian sharing and exploring together which I can ever remember." He went on to say: "Yesterday was for me a wonderful experience. The warmth of welcome from you all, the openness of our discussions and the very exciting and spiritually significant nature of our subject matter all went to make a time that will long be a source of joy, gratitude and inspiration."[2]

Dr. Baker had been invited by Lt. Colonel Street to attend because it was felt that he could bring a wider perspective and an informed academic mind, especially to the Commission's thinking on the subject of the Army and the sacraments. He is an influential figure in Anglican circles, with impeccable ecclesiastical and scholarly credentials. He began his paper by alluding to the Army as a church:

> *I shall proceed on the basis that the Army is a "church"—in Roman terminology an "ecclesiastical body"—not only because that is in practice your ecumenical standing, but also because we could not even be discussing the issue before us today if you were not. It would, of course, be marvelous for the rest of us if we could claim that you were, as your Founder first saw you, a special agency for all the churches, since we could then all bask in the glory of your global good works! But we cannot get away with that for two relevant reasons.*

First, it is the membership of the Army which gives Salvationists their primary identity with the whole Christian people—something that is not true, for example, of members of religious orders or movements such as Opus Dei or the Jesuits. Secondly, what you are considering is not whether your members may, if they wish, receive the sacraments elsewhere. They are free to do that already. It is whether you, as a definable Christian group, are to provide sacramental worship for your members; and to do that would clearly be to recognize yourselves as having the authority proper to an ecclesiastical body.[3]

Next he reminded us that even the Roman Catholic Church was showing signs of considerable movement in their thinking on the subject of sacraments. He referred to two changes in the latest *Catechism of the Catholic Church*. First, it is no longer taught that infants who die unbaptized live in limbo, an eternal state of perfect natural happiness, which used to be regarded as the best and only possible destiny for them, because without baptism they could enjoy neither the grace of Christ nor the Beatific Vision in heaven.

The new teaching is that these infants are now entrusted by the Church to the mercy of God who desires that everyone should be saved, and that Jesus' tenderness toward children allows us to hope that there is a way of salvation for children who have died without baptism. The second change is that everyone "who is ignorant of the Gospel of Christ and of his Church, but seeks the truth and does the will of God in accordance with his understanding of it, can be saved" on the grounds that "such persons would have desired baptism explicitly if they had known its necessity."[4]

How do these two matters indicate a basic change of attitude to the sacrament of baptism? Dr. Baker saw in them "the beginnings of a revolution not just in sacramental theology but in the whole Christian understanding of God and His saving dealings with the world."[5] Paragraphs 1260 and 1261 of the *Catechism* open the door to the belief by Catholics that neither the sacraments nor even conscious faith are necessary to salvation in certain defined circumstances. The Bishop drew the following conclusion: "Slowly, slowly, what is being conceded is the absolute primacy of God's total freedom to act graciously to whom He will, consequent largely upon the changing relationship of Christianity to other faiths and philosophies in a pluralist world. That is the context in which any teaching about, or use of, the sacraments will in the future have to take place."[6]

The Bishop concluded his remarks by making a series of stark, but closely reasoned, assertions:

- Sacraments are not static things, but are developing, sometimes in false ways that obscure Gospel truths.

- John 6, with its Eucharistic imagery, has often been subjected to grossly mistaken exegesis with the resultant "colossal problem for Christians today that the worship of 80 percent of all nominal Christians in the world is built on the mistaken belief that in the Eucharist the bread and wine are meant to become, in some sense, the body and blood of Christ."

- The Eucharist has been "the victim of tragic and monstrous distortion," compared with anything that Jesus can possibly have had in mind.

- If one were thinking of starting afresh to celebrate the Lord's Supper, it would be essential to do so on the basis of "a complete restatement of what it is really about."

- "There can be no reason in Christian theology or Christian history why The Salvation Army should not retain in full vigor its insight that sacraments are not necessary, for a saving relationship with Christ can be had without them—of that there can be no doubt whatever."

• However, if properly taught and explained, the sacraments can be "of immense enrichment to believers."

The Commission's Report

Salvationists everywhere awaited the formal report of the Commission. The members and their work had been the object of widespread prayer support throughout the two years of their meeting together, and the deep significance of their recommendations was recognized for an Army seeking God's will and reaffirming touch as it neared the twenty–first century. General Paul Rader expressed his hope that the final report could be ready for the agenda of the International Conference of Leaders in Melbourne, Australia in March 1998. (This Conference is held every three years and is attended by every territorial commander and officer commanding throughout the world, so that every country where the Army is present is represented.)

Thus it was that Lt. Colonel Robert Street stood in a plenary session of the Conference of Leaders to present the report in an atmosphere of considerable expectancy. In the end, time ran out, for the delegates were full of comments and questions, and the Conference timetable was adjusted to give still further opportunity for debate and eventual consensus on the crucial matters enshrined in the report, which was eventually adopted by the Conference. It is to the recommendations of the report that we now turn.

God–Given Freedom

In promulgating the report to every part of the Army world, General Rader commended the Commission's work and underscored the report's emphasis upon the God–given freedom of Salvationists, who come from every culture and race. It is a freedom to be fully embraced, declared the General in his written introduction. He encouraged every Salvationist to explore with vigor and anticipation the God–given freedom the Army has in Christ—a freedom which, when fully embraced, confirms again and again the graciousness of God and His power to transform lives. Freedom and flexibility in worship and in how we nourish our inner spiritual lives are firmly rooted in the Army's history. They have always been at the heart of our most inspiring and effective initiatives, and they point the way ahead for what God has planned for His people in the Army.

Early in the report, the Commission described how the members became increasingly aware both of the rich cultural diversity possessed by the Army in 106 countries, and also of the unifying power found in its shared universal doctrines and in its common practices. The following were identified and confirmed as integral to the Army's spiritual life:

- Its calling under God to engage in ministry to the unchurched
- The doctrine of the priesthood of all believers
- The essential belief in the need for a personal saving faith in Jesus as Lord
- Our divine calling to holiness of life
- The use and theological significance of the Mercy Seat, symbolizing our mission for souls
- Our obedience to the divine urge to minister to the social and material needs of others.[7]

Though these six central elements are seen as not negotiable, they form a context in which freedom can flourish—freedom of worship forms, freedom of religious expression, freedom of self–expression, freedom to seek a personal and closer walk with the Lord. It was in giving consideration to the practices of other churches that the Commission realized afresh the Army's freedom in Christ and in the Spirit. A settled liturgy has never been part of Army tradition, and the Commission, while recognizing the benefit of this to other groups, recommended that freedom of form should continue to be our emphasis.

Perhaps the keenest interest among those waiting for the report was in what the Commission would have to say about the Army and the sacraments. Two distinct statements were drawn up, one on baptism and one on the Lord's Supper.

Baptism

The essential thrust of the Commission's views were as follows:

> • Water baptism is one valid way of publicly witnessing to entry into the body of Christ on earth, but the ceremony is essentially a confirmation of a life–changing encounter that has already taken place, and is not the encounter itself. Baptism is not the act of becoming a Christian.
>
> [The report appears to assume only one possible model for the theology of baptism, in which the person baptized has already made a solid faith commitment, and so the act of baptism becomes a memorable re–enactment of that step, merely making visible what has already happened in the spiritual realm. Thus the spiritual result is already valid whether the baptism takes place or not.
>
> This accords with a Salvationist view of all religious ritual. Many believers, however, take an altogether different theological view of baptism, understanding that in the very course of the ceremony a covenant is struck between God, the believer being baptized and the church. This view regards the covenant as not made unless the ceremony is carried out, and seeks to offer the believer the assurance that the covenant is authentically brought into being regardless of the believer's subjective feelings (as distinct from personal faith) at the time of the ceremony. The Commission's report does not address this second view of baptism. The Army would wish to

acknowledge the pastoral helpfulness inherent in this teaching, without in any way abandoning its clear conviction that all the spiritual benefits are available as a consequence of faith and faith alone. Outward forms might bring home graphically to our human empirical senses the invisible spiritual transaction, but the transaction ought to be recognized as authentic independent of the ceremony. Thus the second theory of baptism is not one compatible with a Salvationist theology of the relationship between grace and outward forms, and this should be noted even though the report does not address the point.]

• The Army believes, in accordance with the Scriptures, that there is one body and one Spirit, one Lord, one faith, one baptism by the Holy Spirit.

• The Army's simple ceremony of recognizing a new adult member (a senior soldier) is known as a "swearing–in" ceremony. This is the Salvationist equivalent of baptism in that it allows the new believer to witness openly to new–found faith and affords a public moment of being received into the fellowship of believers. This ceremony takes place beneath the flag of The Salvation Army, which by its threefold colors symbolizes the Christian Trinity of Father, Son and Holy Spirit.

• The Army acknowledges that there are many worthy ways of publicly witnessing to having been baptized into the body of Christ by the Holy Spirit.

• The Commission recommended that the wording of the swearing–in ceremony for soldiers be amended, along with the Covenant signed by each soldier, to make explicitly the point that the swearing–in was an affirmation of the soldier's incorporation into the body of Christ and baptism into Christ by God the Holy Spirit.

The Lord's Supper

Members of the Commission were unanimous in their conviction that no sacrament is essential to salvation or to growth in grace. There was also unanimity on the immediacy and directness of grace to the believer's soul by faith, independent of any ritual. A small minority of Commission members, although wholeheartedly affirming these two beliefs, nevertheless felt that it was time for the Army to begin to use some sort of outward sacramental ceremony. However, the overwhelming majority were in favor of retaining our present freedom from sacramental ceremonies.

The following main points are expressed in the report:

- God's grace is freely and readily accessible to all people at all times and in all places.

  [The report does not address directly the fact that most Christians would have no quarrel with us when we say that grace is available to anyone at all times and in all places as God chooses, but that many of these would go on to say that nevertheless God has chosen to be uniquely and extraordinarily present in the elements of the sacrament duly blessed by a priest in holy orders and authorized to preside in the ceremony. The Army has never felt obligated to officially deny or affirm such teaching, firstly because of our much–valued freedom from the tensions created by debating sacramental niceties, and secondly because ecumenical courtesy calls for restraint. Nevertheless, if pressed irresistibly for an opinion, we would have to say that it makes no sense to suggest that Christ holds back, or gives sparingly of, His real and personal presence in the face of genuine faith where there is no ceremony, but gives of Himself more liberally where an outward form is involved.]

• When Salvationists attend other Christian gatherings in which a form of communion is included, they may partake if they so choose and if the host church allows. This decision will depend very much upon how the sacrament is explained or interpreted by the host church.

• Christ is the one True Sacrament. Sacramental living is at the heart of holiness and discipleship.

• The Salvation Army has, at all times in its history, sought to place the sacrificial, atoning death of Jesus at the center of its corporate worship.

• Salvationists are encouraged to celebrate Christ and His real presence at all meals and in all worship services, seeking to explore the deep significance of those meals shared by Jesus with others, and those shared by the first Christians in the period immediately following His death.

• The "love feast" provides the opportunity to affirm one another in Christlike love in a context of shared food and fellowship, and this, together with other creative options, ought to be explored as a means of remembering Christ and His self–sacrifice at Calvary.

• All such occasions should be carefully planned to avoid the impression of an established ritual, and no set frequency should be prescribed.

The Love Feast and Other Meals

The ISLC report reminds Salvationists everywhere that from the earliest days of the Army there has been a tradition of hallowing every meal. This is not merely a reminder about the saying of grace and of giving thanks before sharing food, but is an explicit remembering of the death of Jesus, our one True Sacrament, as we gather with family or friends to eat and drink. Each meal can become an anticipation of the feasts promised in eternity, and an active participation in the fellowship that is the body of Christ on earth.

The report gives no further details of how everyday meals can be thus transformed, but it hints that useful materials might be prepared in due course. These are much needed. Meanwhile, we are free to be creative for ourselves in how we remember Jesus as we eat. So it might be through a simple prayer at the start of the meal saying, "... and help us to remember Jesus and His self–sacrifice at Calvary as we share this meal in His name. Amen." Or it might be something a little more elaborate, with advance planning so that, for example, each course is preceded with a suitable Bible verse and a short prayer. Much will depend on the time available for the meal.

Even the simplest word or act of remembrance at an ordinary family meal, accompanied by true faith in the hearts of those present, brings a closeness to the Lord and affords an awareness of His blessing upon the meal and its purpose of bringing to mind the redeeming work of Christ. A revival of hallowing routine meals in this way will do much to enrich our daily life. Parents will play a crucial role in setting the tone in the household, and may wish to explain and discuss with the children how things will be, ensuring that each child can play a part in what takes place within the home at mealtime.

A further dimension to the hallowing of meals is the holding of "fellowship meals" for believers. These can take place in the church building or in the home, depending on the numbers attending, and differ from the family meals already referred to only in that they are designed for the benefit of the group of worshippers as a whole and would be based on an open invitation to any member of the congregation to be present. The purpose of the fellowship meal is primarily to cement the believers together in their one faith and to allow them to draw strength for living from table fellowship.

The Commission's report offers a list of suggested occasions when a fellowship meal might be especially suitable, mentioning the key dates throughout the Christian year, and also those practical times when a meal between worship services or other activities is appropriate. The secret is to ensure that these moments do not lapse into a mere "Let's eat!" tone, but are allowed to be imbued in a quiet but dignified way with an awareness of the privilege of table fellowship in the name of Jesus, again remembering His dying for us on the cross, and His habit of eating with those who put their faith in Him, and also with those who did not but would do so one day.

Where then does the Love Feast fit into all of this? The report mentions this tradition and wants to encourage it, but does not enlarge in detail. Also known sometimes as an "Agape Meal" (from the Greek *agape*, meaning "love," the love of God for us in Christ), the tradition has its roots in the fellowship meals of the New Testament.[8] These meals were not sacraments as we know them today. They came to serve the practical purpose of ensuring that all the believers were well cared for, simply in terms of getting enough to eat. Those with plenty shared with those who had less. The meal was a means of redistributing the wealth of the believers.

It is not clear how and when these meals were formalized into a sacramental ceremony. However, little was known or heard of the Love Feast for many centuries, until it was revived by the eighteenth century Methodists under John Wesley. Sometimes it involved the sharing of bread and water, sometimes the washing of one another's feet after the example of Jesus. From Wesleyanism the Love Feast found its way naturally into Salvationism. Again, bread and water would be used, and it was an occasion for personal testimony and the open expressing of the heart's desire to know a life of entire sanctification and holiness. The early Army habit was to hold these on a Sunday afternoon.

An article in *The Officer* magazine in September 1895 shows that the Love Feast was by then being used in the Army as a setting within which strife or tensions among Salvationists could be resolved. The article begins by stating clearly that the Love Feast is not a sacrament, but "is, nevertheless, a simple means to a great end, having for its object the deepening, strengthening, and spreading of the greatest element in the Christian religion—*Love.*" The writer continues: "Where sermons, preachments, and exhortations have failed to bring that blessed love spirit as it should exist, the simple application of the Love Feast has, under the blessing of God, brought peace, happiness and healing into many wounded souls in the corps." The Love Feast would thus "assist in dispelling coldness, bringing in the reign of Perfect Love."[9]

Those early days saw the use of water to drink and cookies to eat. First a suitably chosen song, then prayer and an explanation of the purpose of the occasion. The officer in charge would then go around with the plates of cookies, quoting suitable Scripture verses as these were distributed. Others would pass out the water. Everyone present would be exhorted to search their hearts for wicked thoughts or attitudes so that any grudge or malice might be rooted out and banished. If need be, a soldier could approach another toward whom he held hard feelings and could offer to share the cookie and make apology then and there. Those within earshot would be urged to pray for those involved in confessions and apologies, that all enmity might be destroyed and replaced by the love of the Spirit of Christ. At the close of the meeting, the believers would be reminded of the need to treat as sacred all they had witnessed and to avoid any chatter or gossip on the subject.

In modern times we see less and less of the Love Feast as a device for healing rifts in the congregation. Its use has evolved rather as a setting for the recommitment of the believers one to another in shared solidarity in Christ. It is held nowadays in many Protestant churches to afford an opportunity to reflect upon the love of Christ and the New Commandment of John 13:34. This is particularly appropriate on the Thursday of Holy Week, known in some parts of the world as "Maundy Thursday" (*maundy*, Old English, from the Latin *mandatum*, meaning "commandment"). The Love Feast thus becomes an inspirational occasion when those attending can act out their intentions to live in peace and on a basis of Christlike love with all the others present. The actions of taking something to drink and something to eat serve as a silent statement that Christ will be taken as the believer's role model for all relationships. Again, the food might be simply bread and water, or tea and cookies, or a complete meal shared around the table. No sacrament is intended, and this would be made plain at the outset of each meal. It will be seen that conceptually the Love Feast and the Fellowship Meal are not entirely distinct, and it is true that they overlap to some extent. However, the essence of the Love Feast, a semi–formal occasion, is recommitment to abide by the New Commandment, while the Fellowship Meal aims primarily for social interaction by believers in an informal setting over a regular meal.

It should be noted that the Love Feast is not known in every part of the Army world. It is primarily a phenomenon of the west, and even the name itself may not be readily translatable from English. However, there is wide scope in all cultures to develop and re–emphasize the spiritual benefits of those times when Christians come together for food, without in any way retreating from classical Salvationist sacramentalism. The Commission's report undergirds this approach. It also has key things to say about worship, spiritual disciplines and Army teaching.

Worship

The Army meeting, or worship service, is a meeting with God as He speaks and acts among us. In this setting we celebrate and experience the promised presence of Christ with His people, and Christ is to be the focus of everything that unfolds in the course of worship. We worship God the Father, through the Son, in the power of the Holy Spirit, doing so by our words and our actions, involving the whole of our beings. We hear the word of redemption proclaimed, we receive the call again to mission, and we open ourselves once more to the promised life of the Spirit of Christ within us day by day.

Preaching is still the main event in Army worship. It is the opening of the Word of God; its proclamation and exegesis. It is the application of divinely revealed truth to our daily lives. Often preached in weakness or in foolishness, the Word of God nevertheless has its own power to speak to the human condition, and we believe that its impact is independent of the skills of the preacher. These, however, need always to be developed for the sake of Christ.

The Mercy Seat in our places of worship "symbolizes God's unremitting call to His people to meet with Him."[10] It is not only a place for repentance and forgiveness, but also a place for communion with God and for new commitment. It may be used at any time in any meeting, and especially upon the hearing of the Word preached and when all present are invited to make an inner or, if preferred, an outward response to what has been heard.

Spiritual Disciplines

The disciplines of the inner life are essential to the cultivation of our spiritual health. They include solitude, prayer and meditation, study and self–denial.[11] In solitude we spend time alone with God; we discover the importance of silence; we learn to listen to God; and we discover more about ourselves. In praying we engage in a unique dialogue that encompasses adoration and confession, petition and intercession. In meditation we dwell upon God's Word, and in studying we deepen our grasp upon the truths of our faith, and allow these to shape our intellectual life. In the practice of self–denial we learn to control our appetites and draw closer in empathy to those who have less.

The disciplines of our life together include shared vision, shared mission and shared service. We become responsible for one another's spiritual health. We also become accountable to one another, bringing objectivity and balance to our judgments and gaining insight into our own spiritual condition through group interaction.

The disciplines of our life in the world involve the practice of simplicity of lifestyle, submission to duly appointed authorities and practical service to our fellows. Christian service in the world is a self–giving for the salvation and healing of a hurting world, as well as a prophetic witness in the face of social injustice.

Teaching

The Army has a duty under God to teach and train its adult members (soldiers) for maturity of faith, and for equipping for fidelity to the gospel in a secular world. Teaching takes place through the structured activities of the Army, through worship experiences, through pastoral care and support and through the medium of Christian family life.[12]

The report offers a word of confession "that at times we have failed to realize the practical consequences of the call to holiness within our relationships, our communities and our church. The Army is resolved to make every effort to embrace holiness of life, knowing that this is the only possible means by which the Holy Spirit will produce spiritual fruit in the believer." The report is not explicit on the matter of, or need for, new holiness materials for the twenty–first century.

Teaching on the central place of family life for Christians is also a recognized need. Families play a central role in passing on the faith. Yet today many families are subject to dysfunction and disintegration in an increasingly urbanized world, which is characterized by depersonalization, insignificance, loneliness and alienation. The report concludes, "We believe that in the home where Christ's Lordship is acknowledged, and the family is trained in God's Word, a spiritually enriching and strengthening environment is provided."

This overview of the ISLC report, which ends with a resounding call to Salvationists to be renewed in their spiritual lives, reveals a document which touches upon absolutely vital areas for the enhanced spirituality of Salvationists.[13] The report needs to be distributed widely, studied carefully and acted upon at national, local and individual levels. Those who had been hoping for something more radical will be disappointed, not least those seeking the reintroduction of sacramental forms. However, the emphasis in the report on full freedom in worship, on creativity in the Spirit and upon the distinctive place of the Army in the traditions of Christianity are fully to be welcomed.

Part III
Salvationists
as
Pragmatists

A Slave to Sin
No More

I had known him for about five months. He had gradually settled into the life of the corps and, as his corps officers, we tried to encourage him and to ensure that he was not too lonely in a strange city, for he was young, unmarried and far from home. He showed a strong interest in spiritual things and attended meetings with marked regularity.

So it was no real surprise when, after the sermon one Sunday morning, he rose from his seat in the congregation and quietly made his way to kneel in prayer at the Mercy Seat. The Lord had placed in his heart a desire to be a senior soldier (full adult member) of the Army, and this was his moment of assent. I prayed with him, and we arranged to meet to take things forward in an orderly manner.

The weeks passed, and he joined the soldiers' preparation classes, showing keen interest and apparently making good progress toward the day when he would stand beneath the red, yellow and blue colors of the Army's Trinitarian flag and make his promises as a new soldier, all the congregation bearing witness to his commitment and expressing joy in receiving him formally into the church.

Unexpectedly, one weekday, he came to our home. At once it was clear he was ill at ease. He asked to see me alone. A cup of tea appeared, my wife disappeared, and we got down to talking. He pulled from a pocket the copy of the Articles of War he had been given for study. Every senior soldier signs this document, for it recites our doctrines and sets forth the Soldier's Covenant in which promises are made as to lifestyle and the conducting of relationships.

"I cannot go through with it," he said.

"Tell me why not."

"I could sign everything written here, except for one thing."

"Tell me."

"It's the bit about unclean literature," his eyes avoiding mine.

"Yes, go on."

"I'm hooked on pornographic magazines. My room is full of them, all piled under my bed. I can't go past a store that sells them without going inside and getting more."

"I understand. Go on." Officers of The Salvation Army are supposed to be unshockable.

"I feel so guilty and dirty. I want to be a soldier in the Army, but I cannot beat this thing. The temptation is too strong, and it gets me every single time. What can I do? I'm not going to sign and be a hypocrite. I just don't know what to do, and so I came to see you."

Suddenly the lounge becomes holy ground. Christ is there. The guilty sinner and the compassionate Christ. It is a moment for absolute reliance upon the Holy Spirit for the next word, for total pragmatism, for an absence of pious humbug.

"Tell me exactly how much stuff there is."

"A lot! Piles and piles of it!"

"The fact that you are here tells me that God has decided you are ready to deal with this thing. It's too big for you or for me, but today God is going to free you. Is there anyone at home right now?"

"No."

"Do you have access to the yard?"

"Yes," looking puzzled.

"You have to give every single magazine to Jesus. He is the only

Man I know who can look at these things and not be corrupted one little bit. So get them into the yard, pile them up, and burn them as an offering to the Lord, telling Him that from today you will trust Him to keep you pure. How about it?"

"I can do it. Will you come over?"

"No. This is something that for all the years to come you must know you did yourself. Only you can pick up the stuff, only you can carry it outside, and only you can burn it and watch the smoke rise up, a signal to earth and heaven that this thing is broken and beaten. Satan will hate you for it, but he hates you already, so what can you lose? Jesus is stronger; Jesus is purer. Can you do it? Can you do it at once?"

"Yes."

"Then go now, and call me when it's done."

I prayed with him and for him and sent him on his way with a firm handshake and friendly arm around his shoulder. He was not dirty. Like he said, he just felt dirty. He was on the brink of liberty!

Two hours later the call came: "I've done it! It feels great! I've done it!"

"Come and see me again later today."

He did, and we talked some more about pragmatic ways to ensure ongoing victory over temptation and sin, and especially over what had been his besetting sin. I told him he could wait a few weeks before deciding whether or not to move ahead into soldiership.

"Let's see how things go. I cannot ask a whole lot of folk to pray for you about this specific thing because it is private and personal. But I will be in prayer for you daily, and each time I see you I will just say, 'How are things?' If you say 'OK' then I'll know that you are still victorious. What do you say?" He agreed.

He became a soldier.

Last time I saw him I asked the question, and he said, "OK."

Chapter 7
Temptation, Sin and Purity

The Seduction of Eve: the Pathology of Temptation • Falling Short • The Flesh • Perpetual Struggle • Salvation and Sanctification

---

It is clear from much that is said and written about the Army by those outside our ranks that we are generally perceived as having our feet firmly on the ground. To repeat the old saying, it is no good being so heavenly minded that you are of no earthly use. Several years ago, when we were serving in an appointment in Zimbabwe (then Rhodesia), I came across a newspaper article that described the Army as being long on compassion, but short on theology. I felt offended at the time, but not any more. If we must err, it is better to err on the side of pragmatic compassion. It would have been a terrible thing to read that we were seen as long on theology, but short on compassion!

In this chapter I examine our practical attitudes toward temptation, sin and purity. In the next two chapters I go on to explore our pragmatism in relation to those as yet outside the gospel and the wider secular world in which we all live and work.

When it comes to temptation, it is our strong conviction that there is no need for any person to be forever trapped by sin, for there is supernatural help available from the risen Christ. We believe that a person caught in a cycle of sin can be set free by the power of the sacrifice of Jesus at Calvary through the exercise of personal faith, claiming and receiving forgiveness for all past sin, and being also the recipient of divine strength to be kept pure in the face of future temptations. A look at the third chapter of Genesis reveals some features that all temptations have in common.[1]

The Seduction of Eve: the Pathology of Temptation

First, we notice what the serpent does not say. He is never open. The approach is subtle and crafty. He does not tell Eve that he is planning to ruin her, or that he is an atheistic monster. He does not tell her that he is about to rob her of her innocence, or that this will be her first lesson in how to sin. Instead he embarks on the subject of religion. He wants, apparently, to discuss ideas. His tactics are the unchanging tactics of evil—indirect and disguised.

He could have started by saying, "You're a fool to obey God." But no. Instead he approaches sideways, like a crab. It was to be the same with the temptation of Jesus in the wilderness where, instead of an open assault, the tactic was to quote Scripture.[2] The mask of disguise is often one of piety. One commentator has said that if the snake had had eyelids he would have lifted them to heaven!

All becomes clear if we follow the conversation. First, a question that sows a seed of doubt: "Did God really say, 'You must not eat from any tree in the garden'?" Specifically, the doubt created is doubt of the word of God. He also twists, ever so slightly, what God had actually said: "... from *any* tree ... ?" It is all designed to make God seem mean and unreasonable.

Her reply becomes a further distortion of God's Word: "and you must not touch it." Now God is made to seem even more unreasonable, for His Word has been distorted twice in only a couple of sentences. She has shown herself ripe for plucking, and so the assault becomes more open; Satan calls God a liar: "You will not surely die." She is not meant to take God's word at face value or too seriously. God's motives need to be examined. God does not want her to be like Him. And so the picture is painted in her heart of an unreasonable, mean–spirited, jealous and selfish God. From initial subtlety, the assault is now an open and undisguised slander upon the Creator. Suddenly, however, the conversation ends! Perfect timing. Let the poison do its work now.

Eve fights her inner battle. She saw the tree was "pleasing to the eye." The sensate in her was being drawn inexorably into sin, aided and abetted by her physical appetite, for it was "good for food" too. It was also "desirable for gaining wisdom," and so the appeal came also to her intellect.[3] Then, no doubt, the final rationalization that we all know so well—it must have seemed such a *little* apple! What harm could possibly come from one bite?

Note the classical sequence in the pathology of the temptation:

- The disparaging of God's word
- The disparaging of God's character
- The disparaging of God's motives

These three lead to mounting doubt about the integrity of the Creator and His commands. Next comes serious mistrust of God; then the insidious appeal to the intellect and to the senses. Finally, temptation conquers its victim and the disobedient action is performed—an outward evidence of an inner rejection of God and His just claim to be respected and obeyed.

This is the pathology for all temptation. These things are at the root of each and every temptation. Sometimes obvious, sometimes not. The result? The despoiling of absolutely everything. Innocence was lost; the power of wrongdoing assumed control in their lives; closeness to God became estrangement; and they lost their harmony with each other. They were not even at peace within themselves. The innocence of 2:25, "The man and his wife were both naked, and they felt no shame," became the embarrassment of 3:7, "so they sewed fig leaves together and made coverings for themselves."

When Salvationists contemplate the nature of temptation, they see it essentially through a theological perspective, recognizing the universally true insights in the Genesis narrative, insights which emerge whether the narrative is taken as historical fact or as a spiritually revealing, etiological account ("etiology," the study of origins). They know about sociological factors and the influences of upbringing and of environment, but in the end they cannot ignore the individual's personal responsibility for what they do. Neither can they omit from the equation their belief that every one of us has become a sinner "justly exposed to the wrath of God."[4]

Falling Short

Salvationists are realists about sin because the Bible is realistic about sin. We find no coyness in the Scriptures on the topic: "There is no one righteous, not even one."[5] And again: "All have sinned and fall short of the glory of God."[6] The Old Testament is the record of God's dealings with the Jewish nation as they wavered between obedience and sinfulness. In the New Testament we find a new state of affairs with the coming of Jesus of Nazareth into the world. In the Sermon on the Mount Jesus sets up an altogether new standard for determining what is or what is not sin.[7] It is a standard based upon His own person and His own coming from heaven in human flesh. He revolutionizes our concept of sin and sinning by His own personal behavior: He mixes with sinners and those regarded as ritually unclean; He announces that He has come into the world for sinners, not for the righteous; He is called "the friend of sinners"; and He "became sin" for us on the cross at Calvary.[8]

All of this has a direct impact on how Salvationists think about sin and sinners. Each and every Salvationist is a friend of sinners; every Salvation Army officer is a friend of sinners; every Salvation Army building, whether it is a chapel, a residential center or an administrative office is a place where sinners are welcome to come in and where they will experience a friendship house for sinners. In referring to sinners, we do not mean only those who are visibly and obviously living a lifestyle of open self–destruction, but all who have not yet surrendered to the Lordship of Jesus in their lives, whether rich or poor, socially respectable or lowly, educated or illiterate, for sin is no respecter of persons.

In this way Salvationists, especially officers, are supposed to be unshockable. We should not indulge in wide–eyed surprise on discovering a person's past. We should not "tut–tut" when confessions of wrongdoing are entrusted to us. No sharp intake of breath should be made when we learn what is pulling a person down deeper and deeper into sin. And neither should we behave as though startled if it becomes apparent that the sin is that of someone widely regarded as respectable. We have, in our corporate experience and memory, seen it all and are not surprised by sin.

The Bible calls sin a "falling short of the mark." It is a general term, describing not specific sins such as murder, theft, adultery, etc., but mankind falsely related to God and centered upon self. The New Testament Greek words are as follows: *hamartia*—an error, an offense, a sin, a proneness to sin; *hamartano*—to miss the mark, to be in error, to sin, to be guilty of wrongdoing; *hamartolos*—one who sins, a depraved person (also used as an adjective meaning sinful, detestable). Paul takes these everyday Greek terms and invests them with rich theological content. The mark that we miss is "the glory of God" or, in other words, all that He has planned for us and all that He intends us to be, and the chief cause of missing the mark, according to the Scriptures, is that we are "fleshly."[9] It is worth dwelling for a moment on this key aspect of Paul's thought and teachings.

The Flesh

In his letter to the early Christians in Galatia, the Apostle Paul frequently refers to the flesh.[10] He sees it as an enemy to be fought, but what exactly does he mean when he uses this term? Some readers of the Galatians epistle have taken it to mean literally the material, tangible side of our existence, with the implication that the only path to purity is to mortify the flesh by living in pain, discomfort or hunger. Further, Paul's use of the term has often been taken to refer to our sexuality. All of this is far too narrow an interpretation. The New Testament Greek word is *sarx*, meaning simply "flesh." However, few modern translations of the Bible seem content to use this term. The *New English Bible* says "our lower nature," implying mistakenly that we have a higher nature, which left to itself would be intrinsically good.[11] The *Good News Bible* says "your physical desires," but this seems to limit the concept again to sexuality.[12] The *New International Version* says "the sinful nature," a little better than the others, but still not as accurate as saying simply "flesh."[13]

When he speaks of the flesh, Paul does not mean only that part of us which is made up of skin, bones, blood and sinew. Sometimes he uses the term as a synonym for sin. Flesh is an active thing, ready to grasp any opportunity, and in this way emulates sin.[14] We come closer to Paul's concept of flesh by seeing what he regards as its opposite. In Galatians 5:14 it is plain that he sees *love* as the opposite of flesh. This is extremely important. We might have expected the opposite of flesh to be *spirit*, but it is not so. Now we can discern the meaning of flesh: it is the opposite of love, and is thus a self-centered existence, full of ego. This is not necessarily expressed in carnality, but is rather a broad approach to life based on "self-indulgence" (as the *Jerusalem Bible* translates *sarx*). Flesh is thus an absence of love, of self-giving and self-denying love modelled upon the love of Jesus for us.

At this point we can also see the connection between flesh and spirit; for if love is the ethical opposite of flesh, spirit is its theological counterpart. This is emphasized by the renowned New Testament scholar, C. K. Barrett, in his exposition of Galatians entitled *Freedom and Obligation*. Barrett observes also that "for Paul flesh does not stand for some kind of angelic being outside man, who attacks him and impels him in the direction of evil; it is man himself, man who has chosen to be left to himself. Man cannot, in Paul's view, look outside himself and blame his wrongdoing on a being called flesh, other than himself ... it is the inclination or tendency within man that drives him to do evil."[15]

We therefore live in the flesh (we have no other choice), but we can also through faith live in Christ. It is then that flesh is conquered by love in our choice of actions and attitudes and by spirit in our underlying surrender to the claims of God upon us. In this manner flesh and spirit, as already pointed out, can be seen as theological counterparts, producing starkly contrasting ethical results. Galatians lists some "acts of the sinful nature" or of *sarx*, flesh.[16] We notice that only some of these are carnal and indeed are listed first because they are the most obvious and visible. In these, a person takes to himself rights he does not possess and then exploits another's property or person for selfish ends. However, other fleshly sins are mentioned by Paul of a non–carnal kind but of an equally self–centered nature: idolatry, witchcraft, hatred, discord, jealousy, fits of rage and selfish ambition. Often these are found well–disguised in outward respectability, but are nonetheless egocentric. Sin in the theology of Paul is egocentricity, and flesh is our innate leaning toward egocentricity. "Those who live like this will not inherit the kingdom of God" because they are not in Christ and so cannot belong to Christ.[17] If they are ever to belong to Christ, they must first give up belonging to themselves. Then will follow the fruits of "love, joy, peace, patience, kindness, goodness, faithfulness, gentleness and self–control."[18] The world is entitled to look for and to find each and all of these in every Salvationist, for every fruit of the Holy Spirit is intended to be present in the life of the believer in an ever increasing manner.[19]

Perpetual Struggle

Salvationists do not pretend naively that as soon as a person turns to Christ all inner struggles and temptations cease. In one sense it is quite the opposite. Somehow we find that at this point the struggle between flesh and spirit, flesh and love, self and God becomes intensified: "For the sinful nature [flesh] desires what is contrary to the Spirit, and the Spirit what is contrary to the sinful nature [flesh]. They are in conflict with each other, so that you do not do what you want."[20] The things we cannot do but want to do are the good and right things that please God. Only Christ within us can enable these things through grace. Once we have surrendered to the Lordship of Jesus Christ, our knowledge and awareness of sin intensifies. Our increased sensitivity to sin and the intensified pull of temptation upon the newly born–again believer can make the struggle for spiritual survival seem more difficult than ever.[21] But God will hold on to His children, gently increasing our capacity to please Him. In doctrinal language this is called sanctification, which brings us to the subject of ongoing practical purity.

Salvation and Sanctification

The Salvation Army exists to promulgate and to prove in practice the conviction that the only pragmatic solution for sin is salvation, a turning away from self and a turning to God, asking for forgiveness and freedom from guilt through faith in the saving death of Jesus at Calvary. The Army also believes and teaches that after salvation, following on from conversion, it is pragmatically possible, not of ourselves but through grace, to continue to conquer temptation and sin, and that it is not the inevitable lot of the believer to go on sinning despite now being saved. This is called sanctification, and is often referred to by other names such as the life of holiness or the blessing of a clean heart.[22] Salvation deals with the guilt of past sin; sanctification addresses the issue of the believer's future sins.

It is said that if you want to get inside a denomination's mindset and discover its priorities, you should look at its hymnal. The *Songbook of The Salvation Army* contains just under 1000 hymns and Christian songs. Approximately one third of these dwell on the themes of salvation and sanctification—181 on the claims of the gospel and the need to respond to Christ and 177 on the life of holiness and the person and work of the Holy Spirit. Let us take just one example from each group to appreciate the deep truths that propel the Army in its mission.

First, consider these verses that make a response to the invitation from the crucified Christ to come and find forgiveness and rest. Notice the spontaneous amazement upon realizing what is offered and the self–realism in the closing line of the opening verse:

> *Depth of mercy! Can there be*
> *Mercy still reserved for me?*
> *Can my God His wrath forbear?*
> *Me, the chief of sinners, spare?*

Then the confession of neglect of God:

> *I have long withstood His grace,*
> *Long provoked Him to His face,*

Would not hearken to His calls,
Grieved Him by a thousand falls.

The poet moves on in the two final stanzas again to marvel at the profligacy of God, and to come to rest in the Savior's incomparable love:

Whence to me this waste of love?
Ask my advocate above;
See the cause in Jesus' face,
Now before the throne of grace.

There for me the Savior stands,
Shows His wounds and spreads His hands.
God is love, I know, I feel,
Jesus lives, and loves me still.[23]
(Charles Wesley)

Next, examine this hymn in which, by divine grace, the believer seeks a holy life, pure in every aspect of his being. The verses reveal a keen sensitivity to the need to allow the cleansing touch of God the Holy Spirit to be applied to the emotions, mind, spirit and body of the one making the prayer:

Give me a holy life,
Spotless and free,
Cleansed by the crystal flow
Coming from Thee.
Purge the dark halls of thought,
Here let Thy work be wrought,
Each wish and feeling brought
Captive to Thee.
Cleanse, Thou refining Flame,
All that is mine;
Self only may remain
If Thou refine.

Fix the intention sure,
Make my desire secure,
With love my heart keep pure,
Rooted in Thee.

All my best works are nought,
Please they not Thee;
Far past my busy hands
Thine eye doth see
Into the depths of mind,
Searching the plan designed,
Gladdened when Thou dost find
First of all, Thee.

The final lines express peace after struggling, total surrender, and a glad acceptance of the reshaping, reforming indwelling of the Spirit of God:

Now is my will resigned,
Struggles are quelled;
Clay on the wheel am I,
Nothing withheld.
Master, I yield to Thee,
Crumble, then fashion me
Flawless, and fit to be
Indwelt by Thee.[24]

(Leslie Taylor–Hunt)

Although written in the twentieth century, this prayer could belong to Salvationists of any era and will still be meaningful in the century we now enter. What are the key elements in a Salvationist understanding of a pure and holy life? The basic tenets can all be seen if we take a moment to analyze some speeches given in the year before The Salvation Army adopted that name. The occasion was the Christian Mission Conference of August 1877 and the keynote address was delivered by the President, and Editor of *The Christian Mission Magazine*, William Booth. His exposition of the doctrine of the sanctified life that day has been quoted and requoted down through all the years since. Even if there is a tendency today to find his forms of expression dated, the essential truths he was enunciating remain, and it is incumbent upon the Army of the upcoming century to find different, contemporary language for our contemporary listeners without emaciating the doctrine. Booth's language is plain, down–to–earth and, in the best Salvationist tradition, the language of a Spirit–filled pragmatist:

> *It seems to me there is a large amount of uncertainty abroad among us on this subject. Many of our people seem to live in what may be called "an indefinite land"; they are all uncertainty and fear. If you ask the question, "Have you got a clean heart? Has the Lord made, and does He keep you holy?" you can get no distinct answer either one way or the other ... People don't know what is intended by a clean heart, or how it is to be got, and how it is to be kept; hence on the one hand it is not sought, or being, as I believe it is in many cases, obtained; people enter into the enjoyment of the blessing, but being in so great ignorance of where they are and how they got there are easily beguiled into unbelief, and so lose it.*[25]

All this rings true for the Army of today.

Booth moves on in his address to impress upon the ministers gathered in conference that the doctrine of holiness is "a fundamental truth" for The Christian Mission: "It stands to the forefront of our doctrines. We write it on our banners. It is in no shape or form an open debatable question as to whether God can sanctify wholly, whether Jesus does save his people from their sins. In the estimation of The Christian Mission that is settled forever."[26] Booth told them that the death of Christ and divine grace empowered not only for freedom from the guilt of past sin, but also for being kept from sinning thereafter.

He explained that holiness is needed in every part of our being because without Christ we are totally unholy, "from the crown of

the head to the sole of the foot." Holiness is "separation *from* all
unrighteousness and consecration *to* God." Deliverance from sin
and sinning can begin as a partial thing but it must go on to be
entire: "It means a clean heart, being cleansed from all filthiness of
the flesh and of the spirit—sanctified wholly, being made perfect
in every good work, and God working in the soul all the good
pleasure of His will. It implies full deliverance from all known sin,
the consecration of every power and possession to God and His
work and constant and uniform obedience to all the requirements
of God." Next he was careful to articulate mistaken ideas of this
experience. It is not being "without imperfection, without
temptation, or without the possibility of falling." The holy person
has limitations of both body and mind, limited knowledge and
insight and strong temptations. It means "no deliberate sin, an
absence of the desire to sin."[27]

Some modern commentators seize upon this matter of deliberate
sin to minimize the doctrine for the present age. They point out
that deliberate sin is only one definition of sin; therefore the
doctrine as Wesley, Booth, Brengle and others knew and taught it
is of uncertain value in an age when psychology can suggest that
our subconscious rules us and our actions. This is, of course, to fail
to understand the doctrine. By speaking of deliberate sin, Booth
and others like him do not mean to limit their understanding of
sin to pre–planned sin. They know only too well that there are
dark areas of the will, mind and human psyche that the Lord, by
His Spirit, can illumine, and as He does so the believer, prompted
by the Holy Spirit, engages in an ongoing yielding of those areas to
the lordship of Christ. Look again at the words of Leslie Taylor–
Hunt quoted earlier: "Purge the dark halls of thought, / Here let
Thy work be wrought, / Each wish and feeling brought / Captive to
Thee."[28] There is nothing simplistic about the nature of sin here.
The concept of deliberate sin is not a limiting concept; it affords
the possibility of total cleansing by an ongoing process of divine
revealing of inner needs, each subconscious flaw surfacing by the
grace of God, being recognized as unlike Christ, and then
surrendered to the remolding hands of the Divine Potter.

Booth did not spare his audience. He could not help but preach for a verdict, even to the seasoned pastors present:

> *Some of you are old and grey headed, and you have been hearing and reading and talking about this blessing a long, long time, but you are little or no further forward, and, my brethren, you won't be until you trust the living God, and then it will be done at once ... How hard the angels are upon saints that won't have purity. All that is wanted is the presentation of yourself to God, and the simple trust that He does this moment fully save you. This is easy, and it is hard, my brethren, just because it is so easy. If He had bid thee do some great thing, wouldst thou not have done it? Away to Jesus then, and let Him do the work, and do it now.*[29]

We have no record of the response to this challenge, but *The Christian Mission Magazine* reports some personal testimonies by those present to the receiving and maintaining of the blessing of a clean heart. One such witness came from the lips of James Dowdle, who went on to become a commissioner in the Army, serving in the end as chaplain to the staff of International Headquarters in London. He was promoted to Glory in 1900. That day, before the Army was known as the Army, he rose and said: "Since I launched out into the land of perfect love, I have found it as easy to walk with God as to live, as natural as to eat and drink. ... Let a man say that God saves him altogether, and it will make a mark upon the town. There is nothing like holiness to do it. ... I believe this to be the great moving power of The Christian Mission, the lever to move and save the world. Nothing can be compared to having a living God to trust in to save us from sin in the soul."[30] Dowdle might have been speaking of that which is still needed to move and save the world. In this respect the nineteenth and twenty–first centuries are joined.

Bramwell Booth, William's son and eventually the second General of The Salvation Army, also spoke to the Conference. He made reference to some previous hesitation on the part of The Christian Mission about the doctrine of holiness and then continued:

> *But this evening I have been especially rejoiced in observing in the various testimonies that we are at length leaving behind us the position of apologists on this great theme, and I think the time for this has fully arrived. We have apologized for the doctrine of holiness of heart long enough; we have hesitated, I fear, in our utterances only too long, and I rejoice in feeling assured that one great result of this blessed gathering will be that, from this time, both as individuals and as a Mission, we shall openly and plainly and unflinchingly make our glory in our God, and our boast in His PERFECT SALVATION. Perhaps for this more than anything else this Conference will be remembered. God has visited us.*[31]

Here then in 1877 came the dawning of self–confidence about the pragmatic possibility of living, through God's grace, a life pleasing to God in every part. The passing years have seen some erosion of that same self–confidence. It is not, however too late to recover. By this I do not mean the turning back of the clock, or the re–adoption of the same language or forms of expression. I mean that the twenty–first century needs my personal holiness, and that of all Salvationists, just as much as the late nineteenth century needed the personal holiness of those attending The Christian Mission Conference in 1877. The challenge for the Army of tomorrow is whether or not we shall once again grasp with the same clarity and conviction the truths of which Booth and the others were speaking and, more essentially still, whether we shall prevail upon the Lord with equal hunger and with the same pragmatic expectations to cleanse us through and through.

Chapter 8
Going to the People—
Early Outreach

"Fetch them!" • Undiscussable Issues • Case Study • Street Riots •
Pragmatic Motives • The Skeleton Army • Legal Breakthrough •
Vindication • Ongoing Vigilance • Twenty–First Century Courage

---

No church can survive if it does not know how to reach people
face–to–face. Many a denomination's rise and fall can be linked
directly to its capacity to do this. In its earliest days The Salvation
Army was willing to do anything, to try everything that would
bring Salvationists into direct personal contact with those outside
the gospel. For this we risked abuse and ridicule, even life and limb.
We spurned any counsel toward restraint or respectability, for we
knew time was short and the task therefore urgent. Evangelism
was, by definition, pragmatic evangelism. Try it and see. If it did
not work, drop it and try something else. Always remember that
today's success may be the seed of tomorrow's failure, for what
works today will not work tomorrow when both the times and the
tastes of the people change. These principles governed every aspect
of our first efforts at soul saving.

"Fetch them!"

There was no room for passivity. Nobody was going to rush
after the Salvationists and ask to hear the message, not yet at least.
First, there had to be an arousing of interest. Elementary publicity

tactics, often amounting to sensationalism, were standard fare. Going out into the streets was taken for granted as a necessary prerequisite for reaching people. Getting into the bars and drinking–houses was the same. This was "going for souls, and going for the worst."[1] William Booth once explained that the church bell, pleasant sound that it was, said "Come!" but the Army's big bass drum on the street pounded out the exhortation "Fetch them!"[2]

Today there is statistical evidence that of all the people finding a new faith in Christ, nearly half do so as the direct result of a friendship with a person who is already a committed Christian believer.[3] If this is true, does it follow that, in view of the empty seats in so many churches and Army chapels, there are many Christians who appear to have no friends? I hope not, but we need to look afresh at all we do to attract and win others for Christ. As we enter the twenty–first century, is there the same urgency? Is there the same pragmatic flair and inventiveness? Are we ready to take risks? Above all, are we ready to let go of some of those methods and practices that have attained the status of "sacred cows"?

Undiscussable Issues

Robert E. Quinn, in his book entitled *Deep Change*, speaks of "confronting the undiscussable." He defines an undiscussable issue as "one that is important to the group, but is too threatening to discuss within the group."[4] An issue can take on an undiscussable status because of its history of early success, or because through the generations it has come to be seen as a group distinctive, or because the leadership is known to be attached to it or because raising it may be taken (mistakenly) as a sign that you are disloyal. Quinn reminds us that when factors like these dictate an organization's agenda, it is time to get worried and to open up the windows to the fresh air of debate and re–visioning. He is writing from the perspective of business organizations, but what he says about undiscussable issues applies equally to religious movements.

It is not hard to think of some of the undiscussable issues for some Salvationists. It might be the use of uniforms, or having a system of ranks and seniority, or using quasi–military terminology and imagery or our autocratic (yet consultative) system of church polity. It might be the policy whereby full–time officers who wish to marry are obliged to marry another officer or lose their rank. Again, it might be whether we should call our buildings churches, citadels or chapels. It could be the terms and conditions for active officers around the world or the need to make sure we go on paying more than lip service to the equality of women in ministry. On a broader front, it might be the decentralization of the authority of International Headquarters and the delegation of more power down to national or territorial level. (I express here no personal view on these things, but merely list examples.) All and any of these, and many more topics, might qualify as undiscussable.

Yet recent years have seen a marked willingness among Salvationists at all levels not to shy away from hot issues. As we enter the twenty–first century, our God is granting a refreshing and timely spirit of reassessment, as evidenced by the work of the International Spiritual Life Commission and other study groups. In October 1998, General Paul Rader announced the establishment of a commission on officership. The purpose of this commission is to examine and make recommendations on some of the undis-cussable issues listed above.

Until a few years ago, one "sacred cow" in certain parts of the Army world was the holding of evangelistic meetings in the open air. Any suggestion that these could be dropped and replaced with something more effective was likely to be greeted negatively and even with a suspicion that the person suggesting the idea was lacking in zeal! Of course in some parts of the Army world open air meetings had died out already or had never really been a central feature due to cultural or legal restrictions. There are, however, cultures where street meetings can still be extremely fruitful. Everything depends on how the occasion is conducted and what is included. Timing and choice of location are also crucial. Even the weather will have an influence. However, to appreciate the sensitivity of the subject, it needs to be remembered that it was street evangelism that earned the first Salvationists their reputation for pragmatism and risk–taking. The issue is shot through with history and sentiment.

For these reasons, a closer than usual examination of what it cost our forbears to engage in such tactics could be instructive, not necessarily to encourage a universal return to open air methods, though this might suit some contexts, but rather to stir us up to see afresh the holy courage and sanctified zeal that is a central part of our heritage, and to recognize the sheer pragmatism that brought so much early success.

Case Study

In the lecture hall, abstract principles need to be pinned down in reality, and so the teacher will often use the device of an in–depth case study to achieve this. Thus broad axioms become concrete and take on a vivid reality that might otherwise be lost. The students attending the 1997 Chandler Memorial Lectures received the ensuing material with enthusiasm. Clearly, many were meeting it for the first time. It is included here, as a sustained illustration, in order to:

- Share information not published elsewhere
- Give non–Salvationist readers a taste of where we have come from
- Recapture the drive of our early pioneers, with their zeal, risk–taking and disregard for personal reputation
- Show the absolute urgency that our forbears attached to soul–saving, and to reveal again their practical, working premise that their pragmatic God, and the gospel of Jesus, were simply unstoppable
- Contextualize our contemporary strategizing on how the Army can go on reaching the people.

In the rest of this chapter I therefore look closely at the way the Army first tried to reach the people, by taking to the streets and braving opposition that ranged from mass derision to outright violence. It was all a matter of practicality. Wherever the people were, there the Salvationists should also be, and no price was too high. The name of the game was pragmatism.

Street Riots

Even the risk of provoking public disorder and rioting was not regarded as good reason to hold back. On November 23, 1882 Captain Lomas reported to his superiors from the town of Honiton in southwest England that some leading business men were making plans to disrupt the street marches and evangelistic open air meetings of The Salvation Army.[5] They had formed another "SA," The Skeleton Army, and were planning to assault the Salvationists, burst open the bass drum, push the drummer inside it and roll it down the hill. They would then throw red paint and flour over all the other Salvationists and blockade The Salvation Army meeting hall. The town Mayor was reported as holding himself aloof from all this, and so no protection would be offered to the Salvationists. The Captain had been knocked down before, but the nearby police sergeant simply grinned and walked on.

How did Captain Lomas react on learning of the conspiracy? Caution? A change of plan? Withdrawal to the safety of an inside meeting? Not at all! Let his own words speak:

> *Oh! Hallelujah! The town is ablaze from end to end, and much spiritual awakening in every chapel, glory be to Jesus! His name shall be praised! Bless Him! The employers promise the people that if they get saved they will not employ them any longer. But Hallelujah they are getting saved in spite of the Devil ... We have clearly established our right of processioning. The publicans [bar owners] grind their teeth at me, their trade here is shaken to its very foundation. It is a fact that about 6 p.m. on Sunday last there were not 6 men in 23 public houses*

[bars]. *The weeknight services are well attended.*
The offerings are better and if the police would
only do their duty, all would be well.[6]

Episodes like this became the folklore of the Army, passed down from generation to generation and imbibed with the milk of Salvationist mothers. It was taken for granted that because the Army was born on the streets, the Army would always utilize street evangelism. This was particularly true in the United Kingdom, for it was there that the heroic feats of the first Salvationists took place.

Lomas was not the only Salvation Army officer determined to press on with controversial and dangerous methods, and many a town or city was to form a Skeleton Army. Over 60 towns and cities in England witnessed riots relating to Salvation Army street evangelism. In the cathedral city of Salisbury, England, posters went up all over the place on February 18, 1881. These denounced the Army and declared that the entire city had endured long enough the "noise and nuisance caused and created by the proceedings of The Salvation Army." The posters accused the city leaders of having done nothing to stop the Salvationists, and therefore a committee had been formed of concerned citizens who would now act for themselves. The sole aim was "to stop the parading of the streets by The Salvation Army." An open and unambiguous threat of physical violence was announced with a promise of financial and other help to any person who found himself in difficulty as a result of joining the committee and actively following its aim.[7]

William Booth was himself attacked on the streets of Sheffield in 1882. Captain Myra Davies and Lieutenant Mary Fairhurst (age 19) were locked up in Derby Prison for seven days in 1887 for marching and preaching on the public streets.

Pragmatic Motives

Booth wanted to reach the "submerged tenth" with the news of the gospel of Jesus Christ.[8] He regarded the churches as too remote from the neediest and poorest of England's citizens. He felt them too intent upon the intellect and not enough upon the soul.

Salvationism advocated a personal relationship with the living Christ, a visible, almost tangible conversion experience, to be followed quickly by public testimony so that your contemporaries would see that now you were a changed person. To accomplish what was needed, an outright onslaught on "the Devil's kingdom" was begun and continued tirelessly.[9] Its method was to attack the Enemy in his own camp, namely in the taverns and in the places of worldly entertainment associated with the drinking of alcohol, for Booth blamed alcohol for the enslavement of the poor.

The brewers did not like this. Vested interests were at stake. The Salvationists advertized their invasions of towns and cities as widely and as loudly as possible, using aggressive language and portraying the upcoming events as sensationally as possible. Lurid posters appeared, announcing a battle to the death for the souls of the citizens of each place. The main tactic was a march or procession through the working–class streets of the town, plus open air meetings each evening and lunchtime meetings at factory gates. On Sundays, the quietest day in England, the Salvationists would burst out of their barracks on two or three occasions singing songs, playing brass instruments and generally attracting as much attention as possible. The personal reputations of the Salvationists was never a cause for restraint.

Every open air meeting would conclude with an invitation to return with the Salvationists for an indoor meeting. There the inebriated would be sobered up, and the ensuing meeting would be filled with lively singing, powerful personal testimonies from recent converts and straightforward evangelical preaching from the Scriptures leading to an appeal to make a personal commitment to Christ, receiving instant forgiveness and salvation. Booth called his Army a "great Hallelujah press–gang."[10] Opposition was spontaneous. The Army simply declared spiritual war upon anyone and anything that kept the underworld submerged. Theaters, taverns, boxing rings, anywhere serving alcohol—all were seen as legitimate targets for Salvationist tactics. The music halls did not escape, and seaside towns were the recipients of special attention.

The Army developed its own music, based on popular tunes of

the day. They even purchased places of worldly entertainment and proclaimed loudly such "victories," converting the buildings into meeting halls where sinners would be saved. This was business acumen placed at the disposal of the gospel.

The Skeleton Army

It is thought that the first use of the title "The Skeleton Army" was in the seaside resort of Weston–super–Mare in 1881.[11] Soon the name was taken up all over England wherever opposition was organized against The Salvation Army. This systematic disruption of Salvationist activity in the 1880s was both a burden and a blessing. It saw many a Salvationist injured or disabled, but it was a sign also that the Army was touching a nerve. It was usually the owners of public houses and bars who recruited members to The Skeleton Army, supported financially by the brewers. Some such groups went from town to town along the coastlines, supporting each other as need arose in order to disrupt the Salvationists. They also wore uniforms as they marched alongside the Salvationists, hurling verbal abuse and insult and parodying the main elements of Salvationist parades. Often violent tactics were used and on every occasion open intimidation. The Salvationists were pushed and pulled, especially the preachers, and often mud—and worse—was thrown. In Honiton the Salvationists were showered with rotten vegetables, and the women were smeared with cow dung and their faces covered with mud. All this was aimed at persuading the Salvationists to go away.

It was an open secret that the financial backers of these bullies were the owners of the brewing trade. In 1881 William Booth prepared a formal memorandum for submission to the Home Secretary, the government minister responsible for law and order. This claimed that "in nearly every town where there has been any opposition, we have been able to trace it more or less to the direct instigation, and often open leadership, of either individual brewers or publicans or their employees. The plan adopted is by treating and otherwise inciting gangs of roughs ... to hustle and pelt and mob the people."[12]

The Army's tactics offended not only those with vested financial interests. Some thought that religion itself was being coarsened. Booth said it was merely being made accessible to the common man and woman. The Army also challenged the traditional view of the role of women in society, and especially in working–class society, for it allowed women to undertake all tasks performed by men and to take up positions of spiritual leadership with the concomitant duty of preaching in public. This offended many, including the religiously respectable. Others offended included the local police, who were on close terms with the community leaders and thus unwilling to alienate them to offer protection to the Salvationists.

In time, however, the attitudes of both police and those in local government shifted so that opinion came to be split as to whether or not The Skeleton Army should be stopped. All of these things made The Salvation Army's tactics a source of considerable strife and embarrassment across England. It did not help that usually the invading Salvationists were from other places and hence outsiders, while The Skeleton Army members were all from the local community or nearby. Booth and his soldiers represented a real challenge to social order and to the prestige of local law keepers.

The Army was a challenge also to parental authority as the young were influenced for the gospel. Employer/employee relationships suffered as workers were fired for joining the Army. Tradesmen who supported the Army were made victims of organized boycotts and were put out of business.

Thus the early 1880s were years of widespread social upheaval, caused directly by the pragmatic methods of the first Salvationists. No opposition could stop what God, through Booth, had started.

Legal Breakthrough

It was in 1882 that the law of England relating to public processions was clarified by the English courts in favor of the methods of The Salvation Army. Criminal charges were brought against Captain Beatty of The Salvation Army in Weston–super–Mare. The charges were registered by the local superintendent of police, Mr. Gillbanks. The case of *Beatty v. Gillbanks* (originally

Gillbanks v. Beatty, the names are reversed when the case goes to appeal) made legal history, so that even today serious students of English law wishing to learn about the principles governing matters of public order and street processions must look up the judicial pronouncements by the two judges in the Queen's Bench Division of the High Court in London.[13]

Captain Beatty was accused, with others, of "an unlawful and tumultuous assembly" by gathering with more than 100 persons in the public streets of Weston–super–Mare "to the disturbance of the public peace." The case was tried by the town magistrates (local residents of good standing invested with limited, but real, judicial powers, mostly in criminal cases) who found that the charges were proven. The Salvationists were "bound over" to keep the peace for a period of twelve months. This meant that any further such offense in that time would result in a harsher punishment for both offenses. The Salvationists appealed against their convictions, and the case went to the Divisional Court of Queen's Bench in London.

The appellate court found the following facts to be proved. The Salvation Army had for some time organized processions in the streets of the town at Weston. They were in the habit of gathering and forming a march at their meeting hall in the town, headed by a band and by flags and banners. Usually a mob collected as the Salvationists marched along, resulting in much noise, shouting and singing. Captain Beatty was the organizer of the marches. The others accused with him were his main assistants. Another organized body in the town also marched. This was called The Skeleton Army and was antagonistic to the Salvationists. Other citizens would collect in support of one or other of these factions. More than once the marching ended in great disorder, with the throwing of stones, physical violence and general uproar. On March 23, 1882 the Army's procession was accompanied by a disorderly and riotous mob of over 2,000 persons, a crowd so large and unruly that the local police could not control them. The Salvationists made their way undaunted through this mob to their pre–planned meeting place, where a general fight broke out. None was seen to commit any overt act of violence.

As a result of this episode, the local town magistrates served Captain Beatty with a legal notice, copies of which were posted around the town. This warned him that in the opinion of the magistrates, there were good grounds for fearing a repetition of the riots if the Salvationists marched again, and therefore they were ordered "to abstain from assembling to the disturbance of the public peace." Three days after the last march, Captain Beatty organized another in defiance of the judicial notice. Again the mob gathered around them and grew in size as the march progressed. This time they were met and stopped by the police. The sergeant in charge directed Captain Beatty to obey the notice and to disperse the Salvationists at once or risk arrest. Beatty refused and marched on for another 20 yards, at which point he was arrested. His two main assistants, Mullins and Bowden, were also arrested when they attempted to continue to head the march after Beatty's arrest. None of the Salvationists offered violence, and those arrested submitted quietly. The appellate court found as a fact that the Salvationists had good reason to expect an assault from The Skeleton Army and others antagonistic to their cause.

The two questions of law at the heart of the appeal were (a) whether these facts constituted the charges brought against the Salvationists, and (b) whether the notice served by the magistrates upon the Salvationists was valid. The judgments that followed marked a watershed in the English law of public order and came eventually to influence also the law in those countries, including the United States, that derived their legal systems from English Common Law.

Vindication

Mr. Justice Field was the first of the two High Court judges to speak. He took the plain view that the aims and actions of the Salvationists were at all times lawful, even laudable:

> *Their object and intention being to induce a class of persons who have little or no knowl-edge of religion and no taste or disposition for*

> *religious exercises or for going to places of wor-*
> *ship, to join them in their processions, and so*
> *to get them together to attend and take part in*
> *their religious exercises, in the hope that they*
> *may be reclaimed and drawn away from vi-*
> *cious and irreligious habits and courses of life,*
> *and that a kind of revival in the matter of reli-*
> *gion may be brought about amongst those who*
> *were previously dead to such influences.*

The marching of the Salvationists was in itself "certainly not an unlawful thing to do." There was nothing as far as the Army was concerned to show that their actions had been either "tumultuous" or "against the peace." The local magistrates had wrongly argued that if the Salvationists knew with reasonable certainty that lawfully performing their own march would provoke The Skeleton Army into unlawful response, they would thus be guilty of an offense. The fact was that the disturbances that followed were "caused entirely by the unlawful and unjustifiable interference of The Skeleton Army ... and that but for the opposition and interference offered to the Salvationists by these other persons, no disturbance of any kind would have taken place."

Then came the enunciation of the key legal principle, or as lawyers say, the *ratio decidendi* of the case: "The law relating to unlawful assemblies, as laid down in the books and cases, affords no support to the view of the matter for which the learned counsel for the respondent was obliged to contend, namely that persons acting lawfully are to be held responsible and punished merely because other persons are thereby induced to act unlawfully and create a disturbance." The learned judge concluded by warning The Skeleton Army that they needed to learn that "they have no possible right to interfere with or in any way obstruct The Salvation Army in their lawful and peaceable processions."

The second judge, Mr. Justice Cave, stressed the peaceful intentions of the Salvationists and the lawful purposes of the procession and the street meetings. Had the Army planned to meet force with force the legal outcome would have been different, but this was not the case. There could be no support for the proposition in law that a man may be punished for acting lawfully even if he knows that his so doing may induce another man to act unlawfully.

This legal precedent was followed in several subsequent cases in the decade or so that followed, many of these again involving The Salvation Army. The legal principle articulated by the judges remained a part of English law ever since. After 1882 the local authorities began to seek other ways of controlling street processions and many asked Parliament for discretionary powers embodied in legislation. This led then to further efforts by the Army to ensure that such enactments did not curtail their hard won freedoms.

Ongoing Vigilance

For the last hundred years or more the Parliament of the United Kingdom has been enacting legislation, granting to local counties, cities and towns sweeping powers to control street processions, including powers to prohibit a procession, to determine its route and to determine the numbers taking part. On each and every occasion that such a bill has come before the legislature, The Salvation Army has made formal representations to the concerned local authority and to the relevant government ministry at national level, seeking a named exemption clause so that the provisions as enacted would be stated explicitly not to apply to processions organized by The Salvation Army as commonly and customarily held by them. The Army has been singularly successful in this. There are today over 100 statutes in England that give a named exemption to marches organized by the Army. The freedom of the streets has been preserved.

In the 1980s two particular episodes arose which presented a serious challenge to the Army's freedom of the streets. The first was in the form of the Civic Government (Scotland) Bill (1981) which sought to regulate the powers of local governments in Scotland, including their powers over street processions.[14] In 1982 I was appointed to International Headquarters in London as the legal and parliamentary advisor. The then Commissioner Eva Burrows was territorial commander for Scotland and was very concerned about the effect of the bill upon the Army's open air witness in Scotland. One of my first official duties was to meet with government officials at the Scottish Office to negotiate an exemption for the Army so that our Christian freedoms would not be curtailed in any way. Commissioner Burrows was also present and we were given much valuable assistance by our wise and experienced parliamentary agent, Mr. Jeremy Francis. It was not an easy meeting.

The government faced the problem of sectarian marches by opposing Protestant and Roman Catholic groups in Scotland, which often ended in violence. We tried to impress upon our hearers the historic position of the Army in these matters. No promises were given at that meeting concerning a change in the bill. However, four weeks later my telephone rang. It was Jeremy Francis to say that the Scottish Office had yielded to our representations and that the government would now introduce its own amendments to the bill to accommodate the Army's point of view. God is good! The Solicitor–General for Scotland stood up in the House of Commons and announced: "In this group of amendments we are seeking to meet the representations made to us ... principally by The Salvation Army. It is worth recording that the approach made by The Salvation Army was a model of the way in which outside bodies should lobby. While The Salvation Army put forward a strong view to which it stuck assiduously, it nevertheless recognized the responsibilities and duties of the government."[15] Naturally, we were very satisfied.

A few years later, because of political and civil unrest in Northern Ireland where sectarian religious marches were a cause of serious provocation to opposing factions, the British government introduced a statutory measure designed to make all street processions subject to the direct control of the Royal Ulster Constabulary.[16] Under these provisions it would be a criminal offense to march without first having a permit from the police, something entirely alien to the tradition of street processions anywhere in the United Kingdom. The Salvation Army saw these proposals as a threat to their historic right to march and witness in their own way.

It fell once again to the office of the legal and parliamentary advisor at International Headquarters to make known the Army's views to the government through the Northern Ireland Office. Early meetings took place with lower ranking officials. I attended with Jeremy Francis, but these produced no result; the government took the view that the situation was extreme and that The Salvation Army was merely an indirect and unintended victim of measures badly needed for the peaceful conduct of affairs on the streets of Northern Ireland. We explained carefully our religious convictions in the matter, our views on freedom of religious expression and freedom of speech in the open air and our historic stance even at the cost of physical injury and imprisonment.

In the end we came face to face with the government minister himself, but he too was unimpressed. I recall clearly the scene in his office. Jeremy Francis was there with me, and so too was the divisional commander for the Ireland division. The minister was surrounded by civil servants and other officials. When it became clear that the minister would yield no ground, we played our only remaining card. I had ensured that leaders at International Headquarters and at National Headquarters for the British territory (as it was then known) understood all that was at stake and had ensured how far they wished us to go in the negotiations.

I took a deep breath and flatly told the minister that the Salvationists would defy the law and go on marching. We reminded him that we had made every possible representation by democratic means, but that he was now forcing us into an impossible dilemma. We asked him to consider how popular it would be with the voters to see his government become the first ever government in the United Kingdom to arrest Salvationists going peaceably about their business of witnessing to the Christian faith.

A few minutes later, after the usual handshakes all around, the meeting ended. Outside on the street, Jeremy Francis (who shortly afterwards ceased to practice law and took orders as an Anglican priest) beamed at us and expressed his admiration. "You have won," he said. I did not feel so sure. Two weeks later, the telephone rang. It was Jeremy. "They have introduced their own amendment to exempt the Army by name from all the restrictions. You have won!"

It was, of course, the Holy Spirit who changed the minds of those in power. Their ministers and officials saw only the Salvationists sitting before them, and we were not that impressive a bunch! They did not see the hosts of heaven arrayed behind us, or the scores praying that the path of the gospel would remain free and unhindered. Neither could they really understand the profound heritage which was driving us on, the debt we felt to our Salvationist forbears who marched and were battered, and then marched again and again to establish the right to take the gospel to the streets. Neither could they understand the secret and unspoken compulsion we felt, as modern Salvationists, to show ourselves as ready to take risks, even if the risk for us was only incurring the displeasure, for a time, of the government and its officials. We knew full well that the Army held a place of affection in the hearts of the general public that no government could long ignore, and that our record of hands–on pragmatic service in the community, enabled by the grace of God, actually placed the government in our debt.

Twenty–First Century Courage

We began this chapter by referring to the pragmatic daring of the first Salvationists in order to be where the people were and to reach them with the message of the gospel. All this has been examined through a case study of the early day strategy of street processions and open air meetings. What have we seen? We have seen careful planning, with an intelligent awareness of what would reach the nerve of the unsaved and win a response. We have seen a readiness to risk life, limb and liberty to reach those needing to hear the gospel. We have seen a determination not to be stopped. We have seen sanctified pragmatism in the choice of methods, use of the right people and selection of routes and venues. We have also seen astute use of the legal process to defend our cause and vindicate our actions. Clearest of all is the sheer courage of those who have gone before and their utter disregard for the consequences of their actions upon their personal reputations.

Are we like them today? Are we made of the same stuff? Do we have the same courage to risk all for Christ? What are the equivalent risks we need to face in the twenty–first century? Some of them are pretty obvious. We who are leaders in the Army may find ourselves thinking again about the privilege of getting out on the streets of our towns and cities and taking the gospel where the people gather. Where do they get together in town? Do we know? Or are we waiting inside our Army citadels hoping against hope that they will come into the worship services? If we sense the Lord leading us back to the streets with the gospel, how will we communicate? We do not need to copy every old method, but we shall still need to have people who can tell their own story, in plain and simple language, of how they came from a life of unbelief to a life of faith. Again, we shall still need to identify the people in our corps who have the very special gift of evangelism, so that they can mix with the crowd and conduct one–on–one evangelism.

William Booth once said, "Beginning as I did with a clean sheet of paper, wedded to no plan ... I have gone on from step to step. We tried various methods, and those that did not answer we unhesitatingly threw overboard and adopted something else."[17] This was his pragmatic creed. We shall do well to go on following it. He was "wedded to no plan," no preconceived mandatory methodology, but this does not mean that when he tried various methods he acted without planning and preparation. So have we plans for training our people before we take them out, if that is to be tried? The street can be a very intimidating place. Door–to–door visitation can also be daunting, but is still a very effective method when done skillfully. The Army seems to use it less and less, leaving the field clear for the Jehovah's Witnesses and the Mormons who reap the harvest of their efforts. Will the twenty–first century see us moving out of our buildings and back to where the people are—on the streets and in their homes? Will the Holy Spirit endow us again with that yearning for souls that drove our forbears to spurn physical comfort and to pay any price to win even one person for Christ? Will the twenty–first century see our officers liberated from the tyranny of the office, the computer and the desk, set free to pursue their first calling?

Now that *will* take courage, imagination and pragmatic flair, not only on the part of leaders, but on the part of an entire generation or more of officers who have been conditioned to think that ministry takes place in an office between Monday and Friday and in the sanctuary on Sunday. It is time to ask hard questions about *where* we routinely work for God and *with whom* we are meant to be working. We know *for Whom* we work. We work for God, but it could just be that He is calling us from our late twentieth century work habits and unchallenged methodological assumptions, to a twenty–first century outdoor quest in search of the lost and outcast.

Chapter 9
The Secular World

Social Service • A Common Mistake • Partners in Mission • The Massachusetts Experiment • Social Action • The Contemporary Scene • Pragmatism

---

In previous chapters, we considered Salvationist pragmatism in relation to sinful human nature and, conversely, the human capacity for rising to real heights of holiness. We also examined the Army's evangelistic methods with special reference to our historical heritage of risk–taking for the sake of Christ. To complete this analysis of Salvation Army realism, it remains for us to examine how the Army, on the threshold of the twenty–first century, sees the secular world around it and how it perceives itself as relating to that world and its condition. When we refer here to "the world," we are using the term in a broad sense to include the peoples, their cultures and institutions, such as the law, political systems, values, ethical standards, societal inter–relationships, family structures, the arts and entertainment, traditions and so on.

Some general principles can be stated right away. What follows is not an official creed, but this writer's personal attempt, based on empirical observation through the years, to gather the main axioms that can be seen to have governed Salvationist social service and social action in the past and which will remain determinative in the twenty–first century for how we interact with a secular society.

- We believe God loves the world and everyone in it, for He is their Creator.

- We believe, however, the world is fallen and is therefore in need of redemption and restoration to a right relationship with its Creator.

- We believe the gospel of redemption through Jesus is available not only for individual persons, but for the whole created order, for every aspect of society and for all social and political systems.

- We believe the earth is the Lord's and is the product of His divine will.

- We believe that just as individual persons are accountable to God, so too will all social and political systems be subject to His divine judgment in due time.

- We believe that the body of Christ on earth, including The Salvation Army, is called to recognize the fallen nature of the world, to look upon the world with the compassionate eyes of Christ and to witness to the world concerning the practical possibility of transformation according to the will and purposes of God for all peoples in every age of history.

- We believe The Salvation Army has been raised up by God to minister to a fallen world through the preaching of salvation and sanctification according to the Word of God and also through practical compassionate outreach, bringing relief for human suffering wherever and whenever possible, doing so in the name of Jesus, without preconditions and without discrimination.

- We believe we are called by God to undertake this mission in a non–judgmental spirit, recognizing that our need of grace makes us all equal in the eyes of God.

- We believe we are called by God also to witness to the relevance of the teaching of the Scriptures concerning human behavior, both in the individual and in community.

- We believe we have an obligation to speak and act for justice, being a voice for the voiceless.

- We believe we are called to engage in advocacy for social change and that this may take us into the political arena, but never in a partisan political manner or in a way that seeks to influence how others might vote in democratic elections.

- We believe the world groans under its burden of fallenness and will know full transformation only upon the return of Christ in glory.

Social Service

Anyone who has heard of or encountered The Salvation Army identifies it with pragmatic social service to those in need. In many places, this is better understood than the fact that the Army is a church. Our social services have frequently been the part of our mission that we have brought into the public spotlight. Our social programs have not always escaped criticism, but on the whole the Army's track record in this field is widely acknowledged to be in the finest traditions of Christian compassionate and humanitarian outreach. Certainly, this is what Salvationists want to be true. We understand the Scriptural emphasis upon both faith and works, knowing that faith will issue in practical good works and that faith without works is dead.[1] Salvationist social service springs spontaneously from a faith basis.

In 1986 the Canada and Bermuda territory published a fascinating paperback volume edited by Commissioner John D. Waldron and entitled *Creed and Deed: Toward a Christian Theology of Social Services in The Salvation Army*.[2] This was a collection of extracts from papers delivered at a symposium on "The Theology of Social Services" held at the Army's William and Catherine Booth Bible College in Winnipeg, Canada. Its publication met a long-standing need for the articulation of a theological foundation for Salvationist social service. The book is mentioned here in order to encourage readers to evaluate its contents for themselves. Space does not permit anything like a full treatment of the same important themes in these pages. It is essential, in order to understand what motivates the pragmatic humanitarianism of Salvationists, to grasp the theological rationale for what is the most publicized aspect of all that we do in the name of Christ. At the same time we know instinctively, and can state in succinct and straightforward language, why the Army engages in such widespread and large scale social ministry. It is because the Spirit of Christ so constrains us. He calls us and sends us, in the words of songwriter Meredith Willson, "to love the unloved, never reckoning the cost."[3]

A Common Mistake

Social service holds such a prominent place in Salvation Army activities, and consumes such a high proportion of our time and energies, that it is sometimes spoken of in exaggerated terms. One common mistake is worth mentioning in this analysis, for it is an especially fundamental error. I have in mind the assertion sometimes heard—and this from Salvationist speakers—that the Army has been raised up by God for a twofold mission to the world: evangelism and social service.

This is a fallacious statement. First, it fails to grasp that such a cleanly defined dividing line between evangelism and social service cannot be drawn, for in practice the two overlap. Second, it is only a description of what we do, and does not get to the heart of what gives life and spiritual energy to what we do. Third, and most seriously of all, it neglects the twin motivating spiritual engines that drive everything that is best in Salvationism. I refer to *salvation* and *sanctification*. It is true we have a twofold mission. It is to proclaim the gospel of salvation for sins *and* to teach, preach and live out in everyday practical ways our doctrine of holiness. Thus our evangelistic activities are meant to be carried on under the twin banners of "Our God saves" and "Our God sanctifies." It is the same for all our social work programs, which are meant to be conceived, planned and implemented under the same two banners, so that the timeless truths of God embodied in the words "salvation" and "sanctification" function as a formative and spiritually empowering backdrop to every single aspect of the whole of Salvation Army life and service.

When this happens consistently—that is, when we allow our doctrine to determine the shape, style and emphasis of everything, including our pragmatic social programming (every New Testament letter of the Apostle Paul displays this same approach—belief governing action)—we find that we come face-to-face with certain inescapable outcomes.

The first can be mentioned briefly, though the brevity of treatment here ought not to be taken in any way as a mark of its insignificance. To put it simply, it has to do with *what we say* to people in the context of delivering social services to our various client groups. A prime example is seen in our counselling services. What sort of counselling do we offer? Because we are a church, because we are Christ's and because we are not our own but have been bought with a price, we have no mandate other than to undertake and offer to our clients counselling that is unambiguously and unashamedly *Christian* in ethos and content.

This position will not be well received by every Salvationist social worker or counselor, for some theorize that to mention religion is a big mistake and can only serve to increase a depressed client's sense of guilt, and so on. We have not always sent our people to be trained in Christian counseling, preferring to use secular and humanistic institutions that have earned high reputations in the secular world. But we are not of the secular world. We are merely in it. With the crucified Savior, we stand within the world but also apart from it, offering whatever we have of Christ and His gospel of love. We hold in our hands the very secret of life, and yet often we withhold it from our clients for reasons that can be as varied as the engaging of staff who are not themselves saved (see below), or attachment to some pet academic theory about how clients should be handled or even a basic lack of confidence in the power of God and the gospel to change a person and keep them changed.

Christian counseling is not the caricature that is often drawn of a pious, parsonic counselor prating on and on about the Bible and pushing religion down the throat of the client. Neither is it the simplistic notion that all you have to do is say a prayer with the client, if they want one, and all will be well. Christian counseling is counseling that recognizes that the unique person receiving counsel is the complex creature of a loving Creator; that this person is one for whom Jesus died at Calvary; that the counseling must subtly and sensitively address the whole of the person and the entirety of the needs as they are gradually identified; that there can be no lasting healing that does not include a healing of the soul and a reconciliation with God in Christ. The technique does not necessarily involve any overt or explicit mention of any of these factors (at least not early in the developing relationship of counselor and counseled), but Christian counseling takes place consciously and deliberately in the setting of these beliefs and a Christian world view. Furthermore, the client needs to know explicitly that they have come to a Christian counselor who offers only Christian counseling, and is willing, when the client is ready, to go deeper than any secular approach can achieve.

Counseling like this is offered in the name of Jesus, is made the subject of regular and intensive prayer by the counselor and others between counseling sessions, and has as its goal not only the solving of personal dilemmas or the handling of trauma, but also the restoration of the client to the fullness of life that is possible only in Christ. To offer people less is to sell them short.

So, if one outcome of allowing our beliefs to determine our individual and corporate actions is the effect on what we say to people in the context of our social programs, the second outcome has to do with selecting the people we allow to design and deliver those programs. Will this burdensome privilege be granted to just any technically qualified person regardless of their faith stance and worldview? Or will we be searching patiently and in faith for staff who are, indeed, fully qualified in the professional sense, but are also spiritually qualified to be *partners in mission*? This question is going to arise more and more starkly in the twenty–first century.

Partners in Mission

My basic working assumption in this chapter's analysis is that The Salvation Army's relationship to the secular world and its needs should be shaped by our two axiomatic doctrines touching upon salvation and sanctification. It follows that these should mold and inform our social work programs, and we have come to the point where we need to ask some fairly uncomfortable questions about our hiring practices. This is because each program, if it is to have any meaning at all, must be a response to a perceived social need. It is all too easy to mount programs that we like and enjoy, but which are losing their cutting edge, as though we are providing answers to questions no one is asking any more. That response, if it is to be authentically Christian, needs to be born in the mind and heart of a person or persons who know Christ for themselves and who can see the secular world and its needs through the eyes of the gospel and its values. In short, these people need to be saved people.

This is a controversial statement. In some parts of the Army world, no policy of hiring only saved persons has ever been articulated or implemented. One inhibiting factor is that it has been thought impractical. This is another face of Salvationist pragmatism, but this time working to the disadvantage of the gospel and to compromise us. Another reason is that it has sometimes been urged upon us that if we hire unsaved persons they are likely to come to faith as a result of working with us and so a secularized hiring policy has been justified by claiming it to be a part of our evangelical strategy! If that is what it is, it has been singularly unsuccessful in terms of those engaging with us in social work programs. Yet a third reason advanced for not insisting that our social staff be saved is that such a policy would be against the law. This is something that deserves closer analysis, for it cannot be assumed that every legal system in the Army world functions in an identical manner on this, or any other, issue.

There is an old Latin maxim much favored by property lawyers—*nemo dat quod non habet*, which means literally "you cannot give what you do not have." In the world of property transactions it means that if you do not own a good title to a property, then you are incapable of passing on a good title to another person. It is a maxim that can rightly be applied in the realm of spiritual things too. If you do not know Christ for yourself, how can you share Him with others? If you are not saved, how can you properly function as a partner in mission from within an evangelical Christian denomination? These are hard questions, but they deserve an airing and some answers as we enter the twenty–first century, for the future does not promise to lessen the pressures upon us to secularize our social programming.

These issues arose in stark form during the two stimulating, but all too short, years when I was privileged to be the Army's divisional commander in the Massachusetts division of the Eastern territory in the United States. Let me share some of the things that took place, at the same time making clear that I do not claim Massachusetts is typical of the Army across America. Each place has its own special characteristics, and we were functioning in New England, with its famous liberal traditions and its native tendency to resist personal religion.

The Massachusetts Experiment

By way of background I need to say that quite early in my tenure in Massachusetts I encouraged debate among the officers, and especially among those serving closely with me at divisional headquarters in Boston, on the essential identity of The Salvation Army. Were we a charity, a church or what? All the ground covered in chapter 1 was traveled as we explored the questions together. It was clear that, if we were to have the courage of our convictions, the ultimate conclusions would impact our policies. The officers were unanimous in identifying the Army as a church, but were very open with me about the fact that it had not been the custom to put this in the forefront of Army public relations work. They said they would like to do so, and therefore I encouraged them to do it. If we were a church, was it not right to say so? Why hold back all the relevant facts from a potential benefactor? Even in liberal New England, was there not great public respect for the churches and for the Army too, and could we not rely upon the goodwill and good sense of the public?

So went the debate in the early days. In the end a policy was established that we would, as a division, be entirely free and natural about our identity as a church. We took the simple step of having all our letterhead overprinted with the sentence: "The Salvation Army is a worldwide evangelical Christian church, a human service agency and a non–profit corporation." One or two around me thought this was pretty risky, but I asked them to trust me, and promised them that, if the income diminished or if the sky fell down as a result of our being truthful about who we were, I would shoulder the blame! The next step of course was to print the same statement not only on our regular letterhead, but to put it where it would be seen on our mail appeal literature. Our income remained level. What had we gained? A clear conscience and a knowledge that we could be ourselves with the New England public and have nothing to fear. Basically it was a matter of honoring the Lord in our dealings with the community. Considering it was such a simple step, it produced a remarkable "feel good" factor among us.

Before long other issues were out on the table, and one of these was whether we should be seeking to Christianize our employee force as opportunity arose. All shades of opinion emerged, but soon there was strong support from the officers at headquarters in Boston and also from those stationed out in the wider reaches of the division. It was obvious that we would have to proceed with the utmost caution as far as the legal position was concerned. Step by step we worked on the pragmatic implementation of a new policy. None of those involved would claim we got everything right the first time, but here briefly is what was done.

Step one was to settle how far we wanted gradually and incrementally to press the policy of hiring only Christians. It was not realistic to expect that we would always find a suitable Salvationist, and so no restriction was contemplated with regard to denominational affiliation. My closest staff urged that all persons working at divisional headquarters should be committed Christians, whatever their job entailed. In this way we would set the pace for the rest of the division. Also, all employees working directly with members of the public should be saved persons. However, those in positions with little public contact, like bookkeepers and secretaries, would not be made subject to the policy. We felt also that temporary and seasonal staff, such as summer camp workers, should not be subject to the policy, mainly for practical reasons, but also because there was a clear history in Massachusetts of young people hired in this way being positively influenced for Christ, something that had not been happening in any significant numbers among our full-time employees such as social workers or fundraisers. Throughout all this we constantly reminded ourselves that nothing should be said or presented in a way that would make our current unsaved employees feel alienated or unappreciated. Many had served long and worked hard. Our duty of care to them was clear.

Next we had to determine our rights under the law. I consulted closely and frequently with our attorney, Mr. Donald E. McNamee, a good friend of the Army and a committed Christian. He saw at once what we were trying to do and was supportive of the policy. It became clear that we enjoyed certain rights and privileges under federal and state law because of our status as a church, and suddenly everyone saw just why it was so important not to play down our ecclesiastical identity. The results of attorney McNamee's research pleased and encouraged me. It became clear that we had nothing to fear from the law if we did things properly.

There were two main statutes regulating employment law in Massachusetts. One was a federal statute, the "Civil Rights Act 1964 as amended in 1972," and the other was Massachusetts Chapter 151 B, "The Fair Employment Practices Act" as most recently amended in 1990.[4] Both contained certain exemptions for religious organizations and had been pronounced upon by the courts on several occasions. The United States Constitution, in its First Amendment, protects religion from state interference, and the Supreme Court has declared that freedom from religious compulsion, along with freedom to practice the religion of one's choice, is a freedom having a preferred position in the pantheon of constitutional rights.

The relevant portion of the 1964 federal statue reads: "This title [statute] shall not apply to ... a religious corporation, association, educational institution or society with respect to employment of individuals to perform work connected with the carrying on by such corporation, association, educational institution or society of its activities."[5] In 1972 this language was amended to expand the scope of the exemption from merely religious preference to *any* aspect of the employment situation.

The relevant Massachusetts statute provides a similar exemption for religious organizations. It is explicit on the right of those org-anizations to give "preference in hiring to members of the same religion" and goes on to state that a religious body may also take "any action with respect to matters of employment ... which are calculated by such organization to promote the religious principles for which it was established."[6]

Two questions arose: (1) Is the Army a religious organization? (2) If it is, to what extent may the Army hire employees based on religious considerations? The first question had been settled long ago in judicial decisions involving ministers of religion and particularly in the case of *McLure v. The Salvation Army* decided in 1972 in the United States Court of Appeals for the Fifth Circuit.[7] This and other decisions by the courts have established that no church is subject to governmental interference in religious matters relating to their ministers.

A second line of cases has established the right of a church to deal freely with employees in the matter of secular activities. Thus, for example, an employee hired by a church to clean a gymnasium could be fired because he failed to become a member of that church. The judge said: "A religious organization should be able to require that only members of its community perform those activities" (that is, even the church's secular activities). He went on to say that "Congress intended ... religious organizations to create and maintain communities solely of individuals faithful to their doctrinal practices, whether or not every individual plays a direct role in the organization's religious activities."[8]

It was now clear to us that religious bodies enjoyed enormous privileges under the law, but that the Army, at least in the Commonwealth of Massachusetts, was unaware of how this could be used constructively for mission. Considerable legal latitude was available in the formulating of our employment policies. Attorney McNamee's written opinion concluded: "The goal of having Christian personnel is legally permissible."[9] However, he offered also cautionary words concerning persons hired under government grants or contracts. We therefore needed to modify our new policy when it came to positions funded by such monies. We classified the 400–plus jobs in the division into those funded by grants and those not so funded. We then developed two distinct sets of interview questions for applicants in each category. Several common questions were put to all applicants for all jobs, but for those applying for positions not involving contract monies or grants, additional questions were used:

- Are you a member of a church?
- What church?
- Do you regularly attend and participate in the spiritual and other activities of your church?
- Do you consider yourself to be a Christian?
- Are you saved? (There it was, right there!)

We created a new divisional personnel council and appointed

a divisional personnel secretary to oversee the implementation of the policy. We prayed hard about it all and told the Lord that we would honor Him in this thing. How did it work out in practice? Very well, I would say. It meant that sometimes we had to wait a little longer than before in order to get a person who was fully qualified, by which I mean qualified professionally for the job and qualified spiritually too. But we saw some moving evidences of the Lord directing to our doors godly people He wanted to work for the Army in Massachusetts. The Lord honors those who honor Him. It was a very worthwhile experiment, and now it is established policy in the division under the wise administration of my successor, Lt. Colonel Gilbert Reynders, who was strongly supportive from the outset. Territorial leadership also offered strong support, and gave us considerable latitude for which we were grateful.

The personal Christian commitment of Salvation Army social workers and other employees transforms a mere job into a fruitful ministry. Every key member of staff shares an inner spiritual motivation that makes for solidarity and singleness of purpose, as well as ease of inter–relationships in fellowship. The best results come when everyone sings from the same page in the hymn book, both literally and metaphorically! This is vital not only for Christian social service delivery, but also for effectiveness in the sphere of social action.

Social Action

Social *action* differs from social *service* in that it has to do with the causes of social ills. Social service attends to the wounds of society and of individuals, but social action is preventative in intention. The two go hand–in–hand and sometimes overlap. It is impossible to engage in social action without coming to grips with politics. The Salvation Army is an organization that has no politics, not in the sense of taking an organizational stance in favor of one political party over another or even of one political system over another. Here "politics" means not party politics or the touting for votes in political elections, but politics in the sense that the word itself suggests. It derives from the Latin *polis* meaning "city" and denotes therefore the life of the people living in community and all that arises from that. It is impossible to take the Scriptures seriously and at the same time ignore social ills and injustices. Even the very mounting of a social service program to meet a social need is an implied commentary upon the lot of the people.

Social action requires the Army to be well–informed about social trends; it calls for the intellectual work of theological and ethical reflection; it may involve becoming vulnerable to the risk of being misunderstood or of arousing opposition from those whose vested interests may be affected; it may involve entry into the public arena either alone or in concert with other like–minded churches or organizations; it will involve speaking up for those who have no voice or whose voices have been drowned out by the clamor for privilege or profit; it requires holy courage in the members of the body of Christ on earth.

The Salvation Army has engaged in social action from the earliest days. A good summary of what was done in the first 50 years or so can be found in a slim volume called *Social Evils The Army Has Challenged.*[10] It was written just after the Second World War by Carvosso Gauntlett. It gives accounts of Salvationist social action in England (on the age of consent, poverty, unemployment and factory conditions, and the rights of children), in Japan (on licensed prostitution when the Army was no more than five years old in that land), in India (on the treatment and status of the so–called "criminal tribes") and in France (on the abolition of the notorious "Devil's Island" penal colony).

The Contemporary Scene

Still today the Army undertakes to right wrongs, even if not all that is done can be quite so dramatic as some of the challenges in Gauntlett's proud narrative. The Army in Australia is well organized for social action. In 1987, in order to facilitate a united national voice, the two territories (Eastern and Southern) created a National Secretariat in Canberra. This office coordinates all representations to government on issues with a spiritual, moral, ethical or social welfare dimension. Its methods include the submission of written evidence, formal correspondence on behalf of the Army in Australia, personal dialogue with law makers and attendance at hearings and official public inquiries, etc. The Secretariat is funded jointly by the two territories and consults closely with the public questions board in each territory. These boards exist to advise Army leadership concerning social and moral trends and issues. They consist of both officers and soldiers with expertise in relevant disciplines, such as theology, law, medicine, education and sociology. The standing of the Army in Australia is high in the eyes of both the general public and the government, because of its record of pragmatic social service and because it has come to be trusted and respected for its consistent witness to Christian standards in those things that affect Australians' public and community life. Salvationists are often invited to serve on public commissions and study groups, thus making visible the gospel's—and the Army's—vibrant interaction with the social and moral issues of the day.

Canada is another part of the Army world with a good record of engaging in social action. Like the Army in Australia, it too has a very competent public questions board, this one based in Toronto. But the most tangible evidence of this territory's willingness to grapple with social action issues is the existence of The Salvation Army Ethics Center in Winnipeg. Headed by Dr. James Read, a highly qualified and very committed Salvationist, this institution is housed within (but independent of) the Army's William and Catherine Booth Bible College. The Ethics Center teaches courses for students at the Bible College, but is mandated also to conduct research in modern ethical and social issues, to act as a resource to the territorial public questions board and to arrange conferences and seminars that will serve to inform Salvationists in Canada on contemporary ethical problems.

There is no other institution like this anywhere else in the Army. It stands as an example and as a challenge to other territories having sufficient resources who might do well to establish sister institutions, so that an international and inter–territorial network emerges of Salvationists equipped to engage the secular world on its own terms, in the power of the gospel, as they seek to uphold the truths and insights that are essential if individuals and communities are to be what God intends.

The twenty–first century invites us to do more in this field, for it will be a century of ever–increasing ethical complexity and challenge. The pace of technological advance is not going to slow down. As it is, we scarcely have time to understand the scientific details of new developments, let alone the theological and ethical implications of them, before the next development is upon us. If we do not place a priority upon training and equipping Salvationists to cope in the ethical minefield of the twenty–first century, we must not be surprised when we are viewed as out–of–touch and when our people fail to withstand the secular pressures upon them and their faith.

In the land of the Army's origins, the United Kingdom, public authorities and the media have grown accustomed to seeing representations from Salvationists on a whole range of ethical and social problems. This tradition goes right back to William Booth's "Darkest England Scheme" and also to the age of consent controversy, which culminated in the passing of the "Criminal Law Amendment Act of 1885."[11] This raised the age of consent for sexual intercourse to sixteen years and was the direct result of the work of Army leaders in exposing the evil trafficking in young girls between England and the continent of Europe. Bramwell Booth, then only 29, and journalist friend, W. T. Stead, stood trial for allegedly abducting an underage girl.[12] It was done to prove it could indeed be done, and the girl was treated well and handed over to others to care for her. Nevertheless, Stead was convicted and served a short prison sentence. Bramwell was acquitted. The episode earned The Salvation Army a reputation as a socially aware movement willing to take risks and to go to great lengths to see injustice overturned.

There is an office at International Headquarters charged with the responsibility of representing the social and ethical views of The Salvation Army to the United Kingdom government. This is the office of the legal and parliamentary secretary, which functions also as a source of legal advice to the Army in the United Kingdom and to International Headquarters in matters concerning the basic

legal and constitutional status of the General and of the Army in
the various legal jurisdictions found in the 106 countries where we
are at work. It was my privilege to hold this office from 1982–1989,
and I list below some of the public policy issues on which the Army's
voice was raised and heard during those years:

- Prostitution
- Child sex and pornography
- Alcohol sales legislation
- Age of consent for both heterosexual and homo-
  sexual acts
- Family support policies
- Sunday trading laws
- In vitro fertilization
- Artificial insemination by donor
- Abortion law
- Divorce law
- Economic policy regarding unemployment
- Protection of minimum wage for workers
- Immigration policies
- Equal pay and opportunities legislation
- Prison conditions
- Public order and street processions in Scotland and
  Northern Ireland.

It has been found that whenever the Army speaks clearly on a
matter of social and public importance, not only do we win new
friends, but the morale of Salvationists goes up.

In the United States, the Army has established a National Moral
and Ethical Issues Ad Hoc Committee consisting of both officers
and soldiers representing the four American territories. The terms
of reference of the committee require the members to review ethical
and moral issues from a multi–disciplinary scriptural perspective.
Its mission is to research, refine and recommend position statements
for approval by the Commissioners' Conference. This group has a
somewhat more restricted function than the groups already

mentioned in other countries, having no responsibility for public advocacy of any kind. It does, however, have an obligation under its mandate to keep Salvationists and non–Salvationists better informed on official Salvation Army ethical stances. This is a step in the right direction.

Pragmatism

It remains necessary to be in touch with the modern secular world. Salvationist pragmatism will always have a genuine contribution to make to the public debate. To close this analysis of the Army's practical realism, let us go back to an incident in August 1914.[13] The First World War had broken out in Europe, and German U–boats were sinking ships that carried grain to England. The grain shortage caused the bakers of bread to raise their prices. General Bramwell Booth discovered that in one particular town the bakers had raised the prices so high that poor people could no longer buy bread. Booth asked the bakers to drop their prices. They refused. Again, the General acted as a voice for the poor and asked that the prices be lowered. Again, a refusal. It was then that Salvationist pragmatism took over. Booth wrote to the bakers, saying that if the prices did not come down at once so that the poor could eat, the Army would establish Salvationist bakeries in the town and undercut the bakers in their trade. The prices came tumbling down!

In this single episode we see everything that is best about the Army's instinctive response to social injustice: swift evaluation of the damage to the underprivileged; an absence of fear; a clear idea of the goal and how to achieve it; an understanding of what matters most to people (in this case food to the poor and profits to the powerful); a readiness to be a voice for the voiceless; and the will to take definite action to bring about a change in the situation.

Will the twenty–first century allow us to go on in this tradition and perhaps have cause to publish another volume of *Social Evils The Army Has Challenged?* God grant it. Christians have a duty to seek to shape their world and its institutions according to that which pleases God. Centuries ago this same God spoke to His servant, Moses, and told him that when the Israelites reached Canaan they were not to adapt to the laws and customs of the Canaanites. God said: "You shall not conform to their institutions ... You shall conform to My institutions and My laws; the man who keeps them shall have life through them." Then God signed his signature with the words: "I am the Lord."[14]

The pragmatic task, in our dealings with the secular world, is first to understand it, then to have compassion for it and finally to encourage its laws and institutions to conform as closely as possible to the laws and institutions of the One who signs His name: "I am the Lord."

Part IV
Salvationists as Internationalists

Prologue
A College for Every Continent

If ever you find yourself in London with a half–day to spare, think about taking a look at one of the Army's less publicized facilities. It nestles quietly in a suburban community south of the River Thames, and you can find it by train to Sydenham Hill station or by bus from the famous "Elephant and Castle," not too far from the William Booth Memorial Training College in Denmark Hill. Look out for 34 Sydenham Hill. It is a large Victorian mansion with stained glass windows and a small brass plate on the weathered gatepost announcing that this is "The Cedars."

Here is housed The Salvation Army's International College for Officers. You can navigate the semicircular drive and approach the generously proportioned front door with its huge brass doorknob. You will have to ring the bell, but almost at once someone will open it to you. Chances are that their first reaction will be to smile at you, even if you are not expected, for this is a house of friendship. The face that greets you may be that of a Swedish or Norwegian member of the domestic staff, or it could belong to one of the Salvation Army officer delegates who just happened to be nearest the door when you arrived.

These delegates are hand–picked from every corner of the Army world. They represent every culture, every language group and every nationality in the Army. This is truly a college for every continent. A couple of years before they travel to "The Cedars," their names will have been submitted to International Headquarters by their leaders as persons most likely to benefit from the eight weeks of intensive instruction that constitutes a typical ICO session. Once there, they will mix with colleagues from all over the world, will be stretched spiritually and intellectually in both formal and informal settings and discover a new and often surprising appreciation of the Army's internationalism. Friends will be made for life.

I recall my first visit to "The Cedars." Commissioner Kathleen Kendrick, now in Heaven but at that time the Literary Secretary at International Headquarters, had been invited to conduct a worship service one Sunday. The Principal was the then Colonel Eva Burrows. She received us graciously. It was 1974, and my wife and I were nervous lieutenants, but felt pleased that Commissioner Kendrick had taken us along. We were awaiting visas for Rhodesia (now Zimbabwe), and she had taken me into her department at IHQ on a *pro tem* basis, an arrangement which proved to be six months of enrichment and stimulation among some of the top Army writers of that time. We looked out upon the small congregation of officer delegates that day. They were living, tangible evidence of a miracle called Salvationist internationalism.

In later years, it was my privilege to serve as a regular member of the visiting faculty of the College, lecturing on "Christian Ethics," the "Legal Constitution of the Army" and "Being a Salvationist in a Nuclear Age." For thirteen years I was allowed to meet the members of over sixty ICO sessions, perhaps a total of 1500 officers from every land in which the Army is at work. I cannot recall a visit from which I did not learn something new about the Army, or about what it meant to serve God as an officer in some particular corner of the globe. Even though I went to teach, invariably I came away having been taught.

In this college for every continent, the Spirit of God brings together those who are colleagues, yet strangers. They come with high expectations and jet lag too! Initial reserve is soon overcome as all the deep things they share in Christ, and in their common vocations as ministers of the gospel in the Army, are realized. They give of themselves to one another as they gradually open up about their lifestyles, their difficulties and their victories for Christ. Best of all they pray together, in any tongue of their choosing, and it is then and there, in the words of Hugh Stowell's hymn, that "spirits blend, and friend holds fellowship with friend."[1]

"The Cedars" is hallowed ground, for it is a house of new discoveries—about God and His ways, about oneself, about the Army as our arena for ministry and service and about the ongoing miracle of an Army that began in one of the seediest streets of London, England and, within a century, grew to span the world.

Chapter 10
Salvationist Internationalism

A Divine Sign • Still Expanding • The World for God • The Shape of Internationalism

---

"Internationalism" is a buzz word in The Salvation Army. It is often on our lips. It gives us warm, positive feelings. Whenever it is mentioned we respond intuitively with a spirit of thanksgiving to God. We take every opportunity to celebrate our internationalism, for we see it as a very great blessing from God.

Our international Mission Statement calls us "an international movement," preferring this euphemistic phrase instead of something like the plain and simple "The Salvation Army is a worldwide evangelical Christian church."[1]

For the avoidance of doubt, it needs to be said early in this chapter that when Salvationists use terms like "international," "internationalism" or "internationalist" there are absolutely no political overtones. No confusion should be permitted between the Army's meaning and the left wing political dogma also called internationalism. This latter denotes a political creed that has at its heart the abolition of the independent, sovereign, nation state in favor of "world communities." In this sense a person calling himself an internationalist will be taken as having Marxist views and perhaps even marked leanings toward anarchism. None of this enters into Salvation Army usage of the same terminology.

Salvationist internationalism is not a complicated thing, but it is one of the Army's hallmarks. We think globally, simply because the Army is in so many countries: 106 at the latest count. We use 160 languages.[2] These simple facts carry with them profound implications. Our internationalism comes to us today with all the overtones of our past and our historical heritage; it dictates many of our values; it is occasionally inconvenient for administrators; but all in all it is seen by Salvationists as a very significant blessing.

Perhaps no other modern church, save for the Roman Catholic church, functions on the basis of a worldwide network of national churches all giving administrative, financial and spiritual allegiance to a central spiritual and administrative head, with each national body acting not only in its own interests but also in the wider interests of the international body. In Catholicism all roads lead to Rome; in the Army they lead to the office of the General of The Salvation Army at International Headquarters on Queen Victoria Street, London, England.

A Divine Sign

The Army's Founder, William Booth, rejoiced in the spread of the Army beyond the shores of Britain and interpreted this phenomenon as a clear sign and proof that God was pleased with the Army and was deliberately blessing it by empowering its overseas expansion. It was this theological rationale for overseas growth that gave rise directly to the conviction in Booth's heart that Salvationist internationalism should be thought of and treated as a sacred trust from God. This in turn influenced policy decisions in London. Keeping the international Army intact and free from schism was given the highest priority. More will be said about this in chapters 11 and 12.

The early international growth of the Army does indeed contain signs that more than merely human efforts and plans were at work. Expansion to the United States of America can be traced back to the 1878 departure of Amos Shirley from Coventry, England for Philadelphia. Two years later George Scott Railton, accompanied by seven female officers, landed in New York. Less than 120 years later, the Army embraced the United States from coast to coast and from north to south, with a national headquarters in Alexandria, Virginia and four territorial headquarters—in West Nyack, New York; Chicago, Illinois; Atlanta, Georgia; and Los Angeles, California. There can be no American who has not heard of The Salvation Army. Today the Army in the United States is a vast organization, having over 5,200 officers, 36,000 employees, more than 1,300 worship and community service centers and over 750 social service institutions.[3] The standing of the Army in the estimation of the American public is very high indeed, resulting in the annual miracle of huge generosity through monetary gifts for the Army's work among the neediest.

Just as Railton was reaching America, two young men in their teens were finding one another in Adelaide, Australia. John Gore and Edward Saunders had both known the Army in their native England, and in September 1880 they held the first Army meeting on Australian soil. France was invaded in 1881, and 1882 saw India, Canada, Switzerland and Sweden fall to the Salvationist advance. A year later it was Sri Lanka, South Africa, New Zealand and Pakistan (then still part of India, becoming a separate state when India was partitioned in 1947). Throughout the decade of the 1880s more new openings proliferated: Germany (1886), Italy, Denmark, the Netherlands, Jamaica (1887) and Norway (1888).

It is vital to understand that, from the beginning, the Army in these new arenas was intended to be indigenous. Those first carrying the flag forward might well have been British, or at least from the west, but the Army that took root and grew was not meant to be a branch of a British organization functioning on foreign soil. It was at all times intended to be French or American or Swedish, as the case may be. For example, in Pakistan, the Army is unmistakably Pakistani, both in culture and in self–expression, as well as in terms of its legal status under the laws of Pakistan. This last point is true for the Army in all the countries where it is present today. From a lawyer's point of view, the Army in each country is indigenous to that country, being established under the laws of that jurisdiction and deriving its legal personality and powers from those laws.

There is no better way to capture the spirit of these early adventures into overseas terrain than to be reminded of the Army's first step on Indian soil, traditionally known as the Army's first mission field. What follows has been taken from Solveig Smith's *By Love Compelled*, a history—written with much love and respect for the peoples of South Asia—of the Army's first 100 years in India and the adjacent lands.[4]

India covers 1,600,000 square miles, encompasses every imaginable geographical feature and embodies an endless variety of cultures, some of which have a history going back 5,000 years. It is a land of immense diversity. It has frequently been invaded: by Persians, Greeks, Huns, Turks and Arabs. On September 19, 1882, another invasion took place. Four Salvationists led by Major Frederick de Lautour Tucker stepped off the boat at Bombay. The local newspapers had carried reports that "The Salvation Army is attacking India!" The Indian authorities, naturally unfamiliar with Salvationist quasi–military forms of expression, expected the landing of a formidable force and had anticipated trouble. The Bombay police lined the harbor that day! As the four stepped ashore, the superintendent of police asked them, "When will the rest of your Army land?"

"We are the whole Army," Tucker replied.

His questioner gasped and sputtered, "We expected you to arrive a thousand strong!"

As Solveig Smith points out, this Army did not rely on numbers. It had come not to conquer, but to serve.

Frederick de Lautour Tucker (later Frederick Booth–Tucker, the change of last name resulting from his second marriage to the Founder's daughter, Emma Booth) quickly realized that if he was to win the hearts and souls of the Indian masses, he would have to be one of them. He adopted their mode of dress, their food, their lifestyle. Today 22 percent of the Army's soldier strength is in India.

Frederick Booth–Tucker's memory is a shining star in the firmament of those who took Salvationism across the seas. My wife Helen and I were destined to have the unexpected privilege of meeting his daughter, Colonel Muriel Booth–Tucker. Following seven years as the legal and parliamentary advisor at International Headquarters, we were given responsibility for the Bromley corps in the South London division in England. It was 1989 and we discovered that one of our retired officer–soldiers was Colonel Muriel Booth–Tucker.

She was, as they say, feisty! A strong personality, with a personal presence infinitely larger than her somewhat diminutive frame, she loved the Lord, and the Army, with a very strong love. Tragically, her mother, Emma, was killed in a train crash in America when Muriel was only three months old while her father was commander of the Army in the States.

It was October 1903 and Emma had been to visit the Army's Colorado Farm Colony. She returned on the Santa Fe train with a stopover at Kansas City, and was due to meet up with Frederick in Chicago. "Frederick waiting eagerly at the station was met instead by those who brought news of Emma's violent death, when three coaches, having jumped the rails, had been flung against a steel water tower. They brought the tiny pair of red shoes Emma had bought for the baby."[5]

The baby was, of course, Muriel, who went on to become an officer and to give service in India. In her days of retirement I went to pay her a pastoral visit in her London apartment. She was gracious in her greeting and seated me in an armchair facing her own. "Do you know who I am?" was her opening salvo. "Yes, I do," I answered. Obviously pleased, she then showed me her father's Bible and the picture of her mother, Emma, on her wall. I could see the pride shining in her eyes, and I too felt proud to be in the same Army as all of these special and godly people into whose hearts the Holy Spirit had implanted a readiness to go anywhere and do anything for the sake of Christ.

Still Expanding

If the decade of the 1880s was one of rapid expansion, so too were the 1990s. In the past decade, as though in preparation for the twenty–first century, God has opened or re–opened many a door to the work and witness of the Army. We still interpret this as a sign of His blessing. Space does not permit a full account of all that has happened to take us into the following places:

- 1990—East Germany, Czech Republic, Hungary, Latvia
- 1991—Russia (officially re–opened July 6, 1991)
- 1994—Guam, Micronesia
- 1995—Dominican Republic
- 1996—Rwanda[6]

It was the ending of the Cold War between east and west that provided the opportunity to re–enter former communist countries in which the Army once served, but from which we were expelled in the years immediately following the end of the Second World War. It is nothing short of a miracle that The Salvation Army is once again in Russia. Some of our finest have volunteered their time and skills in recent years to see the work firmly re–established.

There are enormous difficulties, especially because of recently introduced Russian laws that have placed restrictions upon what we are legally permitted to do. We are not allowed to publish literature or to undertake any teaching activities. The most direct result of this is that it has suddenly become unlawful to train officer–cadets in Russia. Consequently, our Russian cadets are now trained in Helsinki, Finland, at the Army's impressive "Petra" conference center. No new opening is free of difficulties, and neither must we expect our re–openings to be trouble–free. In and through all of it, God is faithfully working out His purposes and His plan.

This became evident to me some years ago when, as the legal advisor at IHQ, it was my duty to represent the Army in negotiations with the government of the Czech Republic. We were seeking monetary compensation from that government for the assets it expropriated when the Army was expelled from Czechoslovakia in the early 1950s. A third party to these negotiations was the United Kingdom government's Foreign and Commonwealth Office (the British equivalent of the U.S. State Department) because the compensation had become a possibility only as the result of a treaty worked out between the two governments. We began the detailed work of documenting the proof that the buildings and bank accounts we had lost were indeed owned by The Salvation Army. We went back into the old *Year Books,* and the international audit department came up with old audit reports of our work in Czechoslovakia from the years in question.

Eventually we were able to convince the Czech authorities that our entitlement was authentic, but one drawback was that, under the terms of the compensation treaty, the amount we could claim had to be calculated on the basis of the value of the assets at the time of expropriation. This was a tiny sum compared to values nearly 50 years later. It was decided at IHQ that whatever monies were recovered should be put into a reserve for the ongoing benefit of the small, but valiant, group of former officers in Czechoslovakia.

Imagine our delight when word was received saying that the amount to be paid to The Salvation Army would be precisely *double* the amount claimed! Again, God had worked out His purposes and His plan. Little did anyone think then that His plan would continue to unfold in order to take us right back into the Czech Republic to begin again the work that had, against the Army's wishes, been abandoned four decades earlier.

The World for God

The spirit of Salvationist internationalism can be discerned by perusal of The Salvation Army's hymnal. One section is devoted to songs expressing the practical expectation of winning every nation for God. This section is entitled "The World for God" and includes verses such as:

> *Tell them in the east and in the west,*
> *Tell them of the one you love the best ...*
> *Let this banner be unfurled:*
> *Christ for the whole wide world.*

(Arthur Smith Arnott)

And also:

We have caught the vision splendid
Of a world which is to be,
When the pardoning love of Jesus
Freely flows from sea to sea,
When all men from strife and anger,
Greed and selfishness are free,
When the nations live together
In sweet peace and harmony.

(Doris N. Rendell)

Similarly:

The world for God! The world for God!
There's nothing else will meet the hunger of my soul.
I see forsaken children, I see the tears that fall
From women's eyes, once merry, ...
The world for God! The world for God!
I give my heart! I will do my part!

(Evangeline Booth)[7]

These are only a few examples of the stirring words that Salvationists sing when they come together in celebration of, and renewed commitment to, the Army's mission to all the world. Many of these songs and poems were written in our very earliest days and reflect the absolutely literal conviction of the first Salvationists that The Salvation Army was an instrument chosen by God to do what no other had done and to go where no other had gone, all for the sake of converting the nations to the gospel of Jesus Christ.

Today, facing the twenty–first century, our courage is just as real and our willingness to move very rapidly through an open door of God–given opportunity is the same. The initiatives of the 1990s are proof enough, if any were needed. However, we are more realistic now. We do not think that we alone are the pacemakers in missionary endeavor. We have even learned not to use the word "missionary" quite so much, and we have come to see that, while there is a clear role for the Army in any land into which the Spirit of God takes us, we are not the only ones God chooses to use in building His Kingdom of grace. So when we sing our "World for God" songs, we relish them and we mean them, but long and practical experience now helps us to sing them with less of what some would call arrogance, with more realism, and with a due sense of our place in the order of things.

The Shape of Internationalism

Earlier in this chapter it was said that our internationalism dictates many of our values and practices. It will help if we look briefly at some specific examples:

- Salvationists never use the word "foreigner," with its overtones of denoting a person who is an alien, a stranger. In the Army we do not see fellow Salvationists from other lands in this way. They are comrades from overseas, and are brothers and sisters in Christ. They are part of the one spiritual family:

  Join hands then, brothers of the faith,
  Whate'er your race may be;
  Who serves my Father as a son
  Is surely kin to me.
  (John Oxenham)

- We do not use the word "enemy," even in time of war. In 1940 General George Carpenter directed that no Salvation Army publication should use the word "enemy" to identify any person, regardless of their country of origin and regardless of whether or not they were a citizen of a hostile country in time of war. (In chapter 12 I detail the devastating impact of war upon the precious internationalist ideals and worldwide networking of the Salvation Army.)

- Another practical outcome of our international- ism is that wherever you go in the Army world you have a ready–made family. You also have a spiritual home and a Christian fellowship, which will receive you warmly, like a brother or sister in Christ and as a comrade under the Army's "Blood and Fire" flag. There is no part of the Army that does not grow excited whenever an Army person from another territory visits. This may be an offi- cial visit, or it might simply be Salvationists on vacation, or a Salvationist businessman making a trip overseas for his company. All these will expe- rience the same ready acceptance and welcome.

- The divine blessing that has led to Salvationist internationalism carries with it a concomitant ob- ligation that affects evangelical outreach meth- ods in those countries which are multi–cultural and multi–ethnic in their population profile. It makes little sense to sing happy songs about win- ning the world for God if we are neglectful of eth- nic minorities to be found within a short distance of where we have gathered to sing! The Army in the United States has developed a strong tradi- tion in cross–cultural ministries and continues to refine its methods in this field. It also goes on promoting cross–cultural awareness among Sal- vationists. In this the American Salvation Army is far ahead of many other western territories. The twenty–first century will see more and more ex- amples of the reversal of the classical "mission- ary journey," so that Salvationists from what used to be known as "missionary territories" will travel to the land of the Army's birth, and to other long established territories, to lead the way in reaching out to peoples of all ethnic groupings.

• The Salvation Army is opposed to racism and to all discrimination based on skin color or ethnicity. It recognizes the evils done in the false name of so–called racial superiority and stands with those who actively denounce and oppose discriminatory attitudes and practices. We are also conscious of the need for constant vigilance within our own ranks to ensure that our internal procedures do not fall victim to the insidious temptations of racial attitudes. We are aware of the practical need for positive, pro–active measures to guarantee that persons of all or any ethnic group, and indeed of any gender, have equality of treatment and of opportunity within the Army. This need relates not only to differences in nationality, but also to differences in tribal allegiances, social background and educational attainment.[8]

• To an external observer, The Salvation Army's presence in 106 countries and its organization on the basis of 54 territories and commands (a territory is sub–divided into divisions—the Army term for a diocese—whereas a command is not) might suggest the inevitability of a federalist structure, in which greater and greater autonomy is sought and exercized by each component part. It is true that with growing maturity as a movement, and with an increasing self–awareness and self–confidence as an international church, the Army has been willing to decentralize more and more from the world center in London, England. However, to describe the international Army as having a federalist structure would be inaccurate, mainly because of the considerable and overriding powers vested in the General, the Army's elected world leader. (The position of General is the only position filled by an election process, all other officers being appointed by direct decision of their senior colleagues. More and more these days, consultation with the officer who is being considered for a new appointment is undertaken.)

It is not easy to identify or to articulate those intangible factors that cause us to fall short of federalism, but somehow Salvationist internationalism finds its genius in that elusive but strangely ever–present balance between outright autocracy at the administrative center and independence for the many component parts. The key ingredient is a sense of oneness, solidarity in Christ—in calling, in mission, in spiritual hopes, ambitions and desires—which allows us to see ourselves as one Army, rather than a federation of separate Salvation Armies.

There are, of course, powerful factors that could, if we let them, diminish or even destroy our internationalism. These are examined closely in the next two chapters.

Chapter 11
Making Internationalism Work

**Nationalism • Culture • Human Nature • Legal Precautions •
Other Means**

Internationalism may be regarded as a precious, sacred trust by The Salvation Army, but it does not just happen spontaneously. It needs working at. It needs protecting. It needs encouragement.

In order to do this, the first step is to identify those factors that militate against internationalism, and then take counter–measures. This is, in fact, an ongoing process within the international Salvation Army. Among the more obvious dangers are the following: nationalism, the diversity of cultural assumptions inside the Army, human nature itself, and of course—the ultimate test— the outbreak of war. This last threat will be discussed as a special case study in chapter 12. For now let us look at the others in turn, and then at the specific counter–measures the Army purposely takes on a regular basis to keep itself internationally intact.

Nationalism

The second half of the twentieth century has witnessed an upsurge in nationalistic pride around the world. This is a strong and altogether reasonable reaction against centuries of imperialism and colonization, policies that for a long time dominated the foreign relations of many European countries, not least Great Britain. Peoples all over the world found themselves living as subject races, even if the regime established by the overseas power could be described as firmly benevolent. Historians have already judged the age of imperial expansion severely, and there is no doubt they will characterize the late twentieth century as an era in which the inalienable right of a people to govern themselves won universal recognition. "Freedom" and "independence" have been the watchwords of recent generations. As the yoke of imperialism has been removed, so the world has seen the blossoming of new national pride—in language, in culture and in traditional values of all kinds— as emerging nations have taken their place on the world stage.

This generally healthy phenomenon has not left The Salvation Army untouched. Its effects have been subtle but significant. For example, the former freedom and ease with which the Army was able to place expatriate personnel around the world has virtually disappeared. This is both good and bad. As expatriate staff have diminished in numbers, so the international mix of teams working in the countries concerned has grown less and less conducive to the maintenance and promotion of internationalist ideals.

On the other hand, the same trend has caused the Army to raise up and train indigenous staff to a far greater extent than before, allowing much latent talent to emerge, to the lasting enrichment of the Army locally and therefore to the wider Army too. The secret, of course, is to be ahead of the national trend in the preparing of local personnel for responsibilities once carried by expatriates, so as not to be caught unprepared when visa and entry restrictions are suddenly enforced. Many former colonized nations have, for several decades, been producing their own professionals in the areas, for example, of education and medicine, fields traditionally open to appointees from other countries and often the spearhead of "missionary" endeavor. All this has caused the Army to rethink radically its policies and strategies for the deploying of expatriate personnel around the world.

Another consequence for the Army of increasing nationalistic pride in recent decades has been the changing expectations of

Salvationists in some lands concerning the identity and nationality of those who will rise to positions of senior leadership in their territories and commands. Legitimate aspirations, not altogether unrelated to national pride, are now commonplace and have had to be consciously addressed. The international Army has responded well and wisely by seeking every opportunity to encourage indigenous leadership. Officers can, whenever practical, be exposed to experiences outside their own culture on either a short or long term basis and then, more knowledgeable about the wider Army, return to their own setting to take a more senior leadership role.

The days have long since passed when the top leadership of the Army around the world had a monochrome appearance. At the 1998 International Conference of Leaders in Melbourne, Australia, it was necessary only to glance around the room at the 130 or so leaders gathered to appreciate the ethnic and cultural diversity of the group. It was a veritable "rainbow" assembly, in itself an affirming celebration of cultural differences, harnessed and rendered subordinate to an overriding oneness of aim and purpose.

Culture

Internationalism must also face up to the challenge of divergent cultural assumptions in a body like The Salvation Army, which encompasses 106 countries of the world. How can it be possible to make policy for so many places, so many peoples and so many different outlooks upon life and society? How can an international administrative center in England reasonably expect to legislate in a way that will carry the judgment of Salvationists scattered so widely all over the planet?

A trends analysis of policy–making at IHQ will reveal an ever–increasing awareness of the futility of expecting absolute uniformity in all things everywhere. More and more, accommodations have been made to local needs, local customs and local law. Flexibility is now part and parcel of policy–making, with safeguards built into the procedures so that the Army's international ideals, purposes, and identity will not go unprotected.

For example, from time to time the Army produces position

statements on moral and social issues such as abortion, homo-sexuality, bio–ethics, divorce, addictions and so on. When this practice first started 20 years ago, all such statements (to be used as teaching tools within the Army and public relations communications for the media) were written at International Headquarters by officers with specialized qualifications and experience before being approved for release by either the General or the Army's second–in–command, the Chief of the Staff. The published statements could then be adopted by the various territories as they felt a need to do so. No variation in the wording was permitted except in special cases and then only with the written approval of the Chief of the Staff.

With the passing of time, the degree of control exercised by IHQ eased, and many territories began to develop their own position statements within their own cultural and legal contexts, using their public questions boards to do the research and the drafting. It was still necessary to obtain the approval of the Chief of the Staff before a territorial statement could be released. At this stage the Army had both international *and* territorial position statements.

The next logical step was to bring to an end the production of statements at IHQ. Under General Eva Burrows, the international Moral and Social Issues Council was discontinued, and a new policy was announced that left the writing of all future position statements to the territories and commands, with the office of the Chief of the Staff fulfilling a coordinating and monitoring role. General Burrows also offered very positive encouragement to territorial commanders and to officers commanding to speak out with a Christian prophetic voice on moral and social issues within their jurisdictions. With this change of policy, the original, highly centralized control was delegated downward to a more practical and more culturally sensitive level. It was a sign of growing maturity as a movement, but it was also an explicit acknowledgment that cultural diversity needed to be respected and catered to, something that was possible without undermining our internationalism.

The Army has also felt the pressure of diverging cultural assumptions in the drafting of its *Orders and Regulations*.[1] These are issued only on the authority of the General. They govern our detailed administrative practices, delineate the official inter-relationships between officers of different levels of seniority, and control the functions and interactions of the various headquarters and departments. They also define the terms and conditions for both active and retired officer personnel. Devising O&R (an affectionate abbreviation) is a fairly straightforward exercise, if the subject matter is of a purely administrative nature. However, as soon as a more human or pastoral issue arises, the unrelenting pressures of the Army's many cultures are felt at once.

For example, in the early 1980s General Arnold Brown discerned a growing need for a clear and definitive regulation governing those occasions when, tragically, a Salvationist marriage runs into difficulty. A commission on divorce was set up at International Headquarters with a mandate to draft a regulation that could be applied uniformly in all parts of the Army world. It had to deal with the official steps that the Army would take through its leaders at various levels when Salvationist married couples separated and lived apart, or when legal steps leading to a divorce were instituted, and when a divorced Salvationist or non–Salvationist wished to remarry according to the ceremonies of The Salvation Army. The regulation also had to provide for appropriate administrative and pastoral reactions according to whether or not the Salvationist involved was a soldier, a local officer or a commissioned and ordained officer. It was a tall order!

Being a member of this commission was a truly fascinating experience. One of my lasting memories is of the firm but skillfully sensitive chairmanship of Commissioner Norman Marshall, then the International Secretary for the Americas. His mind was sharp and his heart warm. He encouraged us to look at the theological issues, but also at the pragmatic, cultural factors at stake. We were to be principled, but also practical. The issues we were handling were often controversial, and sometimes the debate would grow animated! Our chairman was able to make everyone feel valued and respected regardless of their personal view. It was a great learning experience for a young captain to see how he handled it all. It fell to me to produce a comprehensive draft regulation for the others in the group to scrutinize and discuss. The members represented many different parts of the world, and those that were British had all served outside the United Kingdom.

After several changes, the draft became the official submission to the General, with the recommendation that it be circulated in draft form to all the territories and commands for comment, especially from a local cultural and legal perspective. The feedback was fascinating. Some countries thought that it was all far too lenient, while others felt that the regulation was harsh and draconian. Some senior territories did not respond at all to the consultation process and were therefore taken by surprise when General Brown promulgated it after some amendments based on the initial feedback.

It was then that the sheer impossibility of legislating in such detail on a human and pastoral issue for 100–plus countries and their diverse cultures became all too apparent. Some territories received the new regulation and began to apply it. Some asked for time to absorb its implications. Still others indicated—with great courtesy—that they simply could not see their way to ever making it work in their particular legal and cultural setting. Soon afterwards General Brown retired and General Jarl Wahlstrom was elected as his successor. I recall a consultation in his office during which he decided to repeal the new regulation, but only after a reasonable lapse of time in order not to bring into disrepute the whole system of international *O&R*. It was a case of having to balance the needs of cultural variety with the interests of International Headquarters in its role as the guardian of internationalism, something which was seen as requiring at least a reasonable degree of unity in how the wider Army conducted itself.

Meanwhile, the new General appointed a second group to recommend an alternative regulatory approach to all aspects of divorce and remarriage, and once again I found myself drafting a new directive, as it seemed at the time, for the whole wide world! This time, however, the procedural approach was kept as broad and as loose as possible. This gave birth to the regulation that still governs this area of the Army's life today. It is modified on an ongoing basis in the light of practical experience in various parts of the world. The quest for a perfect international regulation in matters of this kind is a futile one. The best one can hope for is a refining process that will assist in producing a regulatory framework that is less imperfect, and more humane, than before.

Human Nature

A further factor that can bring stress to bear upon the ideals of Salvationist internationalism arises, ironically, directly out of that internationalism itself. Let me illustrate, again from personal experience. In 1975 my wife and I were appointed by the Army to take up appointments on the teaching staff at The Salvation Army's secondary school at Mazowe, Zimbabwe, which was then called Rhodesia. We were excited about this.

After a journey of two weeks at sea, then three days and nights on a train from Cape Town, South Africa to Salisbury, Rhodesia, we reached our destination, with our small son, Matthew. We had always known about the need to have a global outlook as Salvationists and had read widely about Army history and Army ministry in many parts of the world. Now we were to be a part of that ourselves.

We hit the ground, as they say, running! We left the train at 7 a.m. on the day of arrival. By 10 a.m. I had started work in the Vice Principal's office, my working base for the next 30 months. We were the only British staff at the school, although some time later a British lay–worker joined us. The other expatriate staff consisted of three Australian officers, one Dutch officer, one American officer and two non–officers from New Zealand. Everyone was friendly, well–intentioned and clearly committed to the work. This expatriate group, representing five nationalities, worked alongside well–qualified indigenous Rhodesian (Zimbabwean) teaching staff, all of African ethnic origin, who were themselves sub–divided into tribal groupings of Shona and Matabele. The 400–plus students in the school were mostly Shona, with a minority of Matabele.

We had never travelled beyond the shores of the United

Kingdom before making this journey. I was 29 and my wife, Helen, was 26. We were terribly inexperienced. Internationalism had brought us to this place to serve, minister and learn. We had to: relate to officer colleagues who were from an array of different cultural backgrounds (the differences being disguised, but made no less real, by the common English language); grasp all things African and Rhodesian (including the volatile and violent politics of that land in the mid 1970s); learn new jobs; get used to the total absence of all things familiar; come to terms with the prospect of not seeing our loved ones for five years; and generally cope with the harsh realities of culture shock.

It serves no useful purpose to pretend that being thrown into such a situation was stress–free. Everyone felt it. There were moments of real tension, though none of them lasting or permanently damaging. Everyone had to learn quickly how to live in an institutional community out in the middle of the African bush. For each of the people involved, God was working out His purposes. He was testing us and teaching us.

The years that have followed have seen us appointed to serve on three other continents where the Africa experience has paid rich dividends. The adjusting skills learned at Mazowe have been a priceless asset ever since. Given the opportunity, we would do it all over again, only better of course, despite the strains and stresses. There were many other compensations in those first years at the school that transformed our human failings and allowed us to knit together as an effective and mutually supportive team for Christ and the betterment of the young men entrusted to our care.

The point is, however, that no one should look at Salvationist internationalism through rose–colored, idealistic or sentimental spectacles, for it can sometimes mean in practice that people are placed in positions entailing enormous personal stress. When this happens the only way through is to rely entirely upon the grace of God to help you. I want to testify that this has worked for me and for my loved ones in Africa, in Boston, Massachusetts and is still working for us in Lahore, Pakistan. Grace is at the heart of inter-nationalism, and added grace is the portion of those whose lives and service have been directly impacted by it.

However, the potential for stress does not end with the completion of the acclimatization and adapting processes in the new environment. It can all start up again upon being told to pack up and leave for home. Re–entry into one's own cultural setting is not always problem–free. Serving in another culture changes a person forever, so fitting into the old surroundings again may not prove easy. The Army recognizes this "reverse culture shock," and has published a most helpful and perceptive short volume entitled *Crossing Cultures: How to Manage the Stress of Re–Entry*. In his Foreword to the book, General Paul Rader says this:

> *Cross–cultural service is a priceless privilege and wonderfully enriching experience, but it is not without its costs. Generally speaking, those who have served abroad are resilient and adaptive. Even so, the pain they experience on returning can be disorienting and sometimes damaging. Facilitating their transition back into their home culture is in everyone's interests. It reduces unnecessary trauma, enhances their capacity to function effectively at home, and increases the likelihood of the officer or lay–worker being available for future opportunities across cultural divides.*[1]

Legal Precautions

It has already been emphasized that the task of keeping the international Salvation Army intact is seen as a sacred trust from God. Salvationists believe that God will help them to do this. They believe God's will is for the worldwide Army to be as united as it can possibly be.

They are also, however, people with their feet on the ground when it comes to human nature (see Part Three on Salvationist pragmatism). Consequently, certain practical legal safeguards are built into Army procedures with the explicit aim of securely maintaining the international solidarity of the Army. Because these measures are seldom placed in the spotlight, I have provided a short description of each.

- Legal Constitutions: The Army is publicly registered as a legal body in each country in which it
  works. The style of the local constitution will
  vary from one legal system to another. In many
  countries we have created ourselves as corpora-
  tions with boards of directors. In others we are a
  charitable trust with duly appointed trustees. In
  some we are both a corporation and a charitable
  trust. In some places the Army is registered as a
  religious society or association, in others as a
  philanthropic association. Sometimes the Army's
  constitution is established by an act of a local
  parliament, bringing the force and authority of
  legislation to our status under the law.

  Whatever the form of the constitution, there
  are certain key elements that are always built into
  its provisions. One of these is a statement of the
  Army's doctrines. Another, and for the purposes
  of this chapter it is the key element, is the explicit linking of each legal constitution with the
  office of the General. The General is always given
  a pivotal role in a local constitution.

  It might be provided for example that, where
  the Salvation Army is a corporation, the chairman of the board of directors (usually the territorial commander) cannot take office without
  written proof from the General of The Salvation
  Army that he holds a certain leadership position
  in that country. Similar provisions may apply to
  other members of the board. Sometimes it is laid
  down that no changes can be made to the constitution without the prior written consent of

the General. The constitution may provide that the General shall be a "corporation sole" in that country (a "corporation sole" is a device used to separate an individual office holder from the office itself so that, if the individual in office dies or resigns, the office itself continues in perpetuity and is not dependent for its life upon the life or length of tenure of the office holder). In these cases the General will be free under the constitution to grant a power of attorney to the local territorial commander so the local leader can carry out all lawful acts and transactions needed by the Army in the name of the General. Such a power of attorney can be withdrawn at will.

These few examples serve to show how the authority of the General is built into a local legal constitution so that, in the unlikely event of a serious problem arising, the General can take immediate steps to withdraw a local leader's powers or step in to exercise those powers in person.

- Commissions and Bonds: All territorial commanders and officers commanding receive their appointments on explicitly stated legal terms and conditions. These are set down in a commission, a legal document signed by the General under legal seal in the presence of a witness. The documentary counterpart of the commission is a bond, which is signed by the officer to whom the commission is issued and sent back for safekeeping to the General.

The commission states the following:

1) It appoints the recipient to a given position in the Army

2) It empowers the recipient to exercise the prerogatives of that appointment

3) It places the recipient under "the oversight, direction and control of the General of The Salvation Army"

4) It reserves to the General the legal right to suspend or cancel the commission and, thereby, the appointment at any time.

The bond places on record the following:

1) The appointee's acceptance of the terms of the appointment

2) The appointee's pledge of allegiance to the General and any successor as General

3) The appointee's promise to obey, carry out and enforce international *Orders and Regulations*

4) The appointee's promise to conform to the terms of the "Memorandum of Appointment."

• The Memorandum of Appointment: This is a key working tool for all territorial commanders. A supplement to *Orders and Regulations for Territorial Commanders (TC) and Chief Secretaries (CS)*,[2] it sets down in detail the powers and responsibilities of the leader within the particular territory. Its terms, where these conflict with *O&R for TCs and CSs*, take precedence over the other.

Matters dealt with in the memorandum include such things as the leader's powers to promote officers, spending limits granted to the leader and any matter requiring special provision because of local cultural circumstances. For instance, here in Pakistan, the Moslem and South Asian culture has led to certain expectations as to how marriages will be arranged. Because of this the territorial commander's memorandum of appointment provides that most of the normal international regulations on the engagement and marriage of officers shall not apply in the Pakistan territory. Instead the territorial commander is granted the highly unusual prerogative of pointing out to single officers such partners as are likely to promote their happiness and holiness and to help them in their work.

The contents of the memorandum, plus the terms of the commission and the reciprocal bond, plus all that is contained in *O&R for TCs and CSs*—these, when taken together, define the formal and legal relationship between a senior officer at territorial level and the General of The Salvation Army. It all serves to pin things down in the legal sense and to keep the international Army intact.

- The High Council: The international constitution of The Salvation Army is to be found in the provisions of the "Salvation Army Act 1980, a Statute of the United Kingdom Parliament."[3] (The reasons for International Headquarters being in England are entirely historical, and there are no compelling legal reasons why it should not be elsewhere. Similarly, the fact that the Army's international constitution derives from an act of the United Kingdom Parliament is explained by reference to Army history and does not imply that the law of the United Kingdom has any special advantage over other legal systems.) Among the numerous items covered in the statute are the rules governing the conven-

ing and conducting of a High Council, the body
that is legally empowered to elect each General
of The Salvation Army.

Although the act does not require it, a tradition has arisen at High Councils whereby all
those present, having elected the person who will
take office as the next General, will sign their
name to a Deed of Loyalty, in which each signer
pledges loyalty and support to the General–Elect
for the period of time that person holds the office of General. Those signing represent every
corner of the Army world. This deed may not be
legally enforceable in the strictest sense, but it is
one more device which gives visible and tangible
reinforcement to the internationalism and the
solidarity of a multi–national Army.

• Official Legal Advisors: Each territory and command has an official legal advisor. This qualified
lawyer, or firm of lawyers, is appointed as the
official legal consultant to the Army in a particular country on the recommendation of the
territorial commander and with the approval of
International Headquarters. A territory, or command, is not free to change its official legal consultant without the approval of International
Headquarters. This is a further precaution against
the highly remote possibility of schism. Similar
arrangements cover appointment of a territory's
official external auditors, for the sensible safe-
guarding of the Army's fiscal affairs.

Over and above these formal, legal mechanisms several other
means are employed to encourage and foster Salvationist unity
within a context of internationalism. These are listed briefly below.

Other Means

- A semi–flexible policy is followed with regard to the top two positions in each territory and command. The aim is to have one of these filled by an indigenous officer and the other by an expatriate officer. Sometimes pragmatic considerations render this impossible. If there are several territories within the borders of one large country, as for example in the case of the United States or India, an attempt will be made to have the territorial commander from one of these territories and the chief secretary from another, even though these colleagues may be of the same nationality.

- Recent years have witnessed the steady internationalizing of officer personnel at IHQ. Conscious efforts are now made to ensure as much ethnic diversity and international representation as possible in the staff appointed to administrative responsibilities there. This is an important aspect of our internationalism because of the signal it sends out to the whole of the Army world.

- The Prologue to Part Four featured the International College for Officers. This establishment has a vital, strategic role in fostering deeper understanding among officers of the Army's internationalist heritage. Its contribution in the twenty–first century could be even more crucial.

- At International Headquarters there are senior officers functioning as zonal international secretaries (for South Asia, the Americas and Caribbean, Africa, Europe and the South Pacific and

East Asia). These officers serve as channels of communication between the territories and commands on the one hand and the offices of the General and the Chief of the Staff on the other, making known the needs of the countries within each zone. The international secretaries give oversight to, and coordinate, the work in their respective areas.

• Zonal Conferences are regularly held to plan and coordinate the work and mission in each geographical zone. These are attended by the top leaders in each territory and command within the zone, and are organized and presided over by the relevant international secretary. The General and/or the Chief of the Staff attend.

• An International Conference of Leaders is held approximately every three years. The General presides, supported by the Chief of the Staff. Every territorial commander and officer commanding, with each spouse, is present, as are all the commissioners holding appointments at International Headquarters.

• The Advisory Council to the General fulfills a highly significant role in assisting in the formulation of international policy. Its members consist of selected commissioners stationed at IHQ, but also of commissioners from overseas, thus ensuring adequate international input into the deliberations.

• International events ensure ample opportunity for multi–cultural praise and worship experi-

ences, youth rallies, special seminars, study
groups, exchange visits, etc.

• Within the limitations imposed by immigration
policies of the various governments, the Army
seeks actively to promote the interchange of officer personnel between territories. Officers privileged to have this experience are thus exposed
to life and service in a culture not their own.

The mechanisms and procedures described in this chapter
represent the main ways by which The Salvation Army works to
preserve its international ethos. Though internationalism is a gift
from God, and even though there is a joyful spontaneity at its heart,
like a tender plant it needs to be protected, fed and watered.

Of all the forces that work against Salvationist international
unity, it is the outbreak of war that strikes with the fiercest fist. In
the concluding chapter of this analysis for the twenty–first century
I describe and assess the trauma of widespread warfare for a church
that sees its international solidarity as a blessing, a sacred trust from
God. War provides the ultimate test for a worldwide Army.

Chapter 12
Internationalism in Wartime

War in South Africa, 1899 • The First World War, 1914 • Evangeline Booth's American Army • Divergence Elsewhere • 1939: World Conflict Again! • Internationalism and Nazi Germany • Pearl Harbor • The Neutrality Policy

---

War on a world–wide scale has twice erupted in the twentieth century. Twice it has threatened to rip apart the international Salvation Army.[1] The first bitter taste of war came just as the nineteenth century was closing. It occurred in 1899 with the outbreak of war between Britain and the Boers in South Africa. Suddenly, Salvationists were facing one another on the battlefield. The instinctive internationalism of William Booth and his Army, only 21 years old, was to undergo a dreadful testing that no one wanted. What happened on a relatively small scale in the Boer War was to re–emerge traumatically on a global scale in 1914 and 1939.

On his deathbed in 1912 William Booth said to his son, Bramwell, "I have been thinking of all nations and peoples as one family."[2] It was his last coherent conversation with the young man who was to take over the reins of an international Army. He taught his son well, for in his wartime Christmas message to all Salvationists in 1915 Bramwell wrote, "Every land is my fatherland, for all lands are my Father's."[3] Statements such as these embodied the deep conviction that Salvationists were firstly citizens of the world and only thereafter citizens of their own countries.

Internationalism was, and still is, a fine and high ideal, but has proven itself to be a two–edged sword. Frederick Coutts, later the sixth General, put it succinctly when he wrote, "The Army's internationalism is its crown of glory in peacetime, but in war it becomes a crown of thorns."[4]

Not only were Salvationists thrown into battle on opposing sides, but as political and diplomatic ties between the nations were destroyed, so too were severed many of the links that hold the territories of the Army intact as an international network. International Headquarters, heavily conscious of its internationalist obligations, tried valiantly to articulate, and become a model of, political neutrality, lest any part of the Army's global family should think that it had been coldly abandoned to its fate. A neutral stance was not something the principal western territories were willing to attempt. They would not, could not and did not do it. As a result, the Army faced not only the disastrous impact of hostilities between the fighting countries, but also the unprecedented phenomenon of open divergence by certain territories from the official policy position of IHQ.

War in South Africa, 1899

It was only 16 short years prior to the onset of the Boer War that the Army began work in South Africa. By 1899, 21 corps had been opened, and there were 50 active officers, most of them born in South Africa.[5] With the war not one week old, IHQ published clear guidance for all Salvationists, whether in Britain or in South Africa. This was the first ever *War Cry* article on Salvationism and warfare. It was to be the forerunner of many such writings between 1899 and 1945. Entitled "How Must Salvation Soldiers Act During War?" it carried no writer's name. The instructions were as follows:

> • Never encourage the spirit of war, for there has hardly ever been a just cause making violence morally acceptable.
> • Never take sides, for British and Boer alike are our brothers and sisters.

- Avoid sensational accounts of war and also conversations that dwell upon war reports.
- Pray unceasingly for the war to stop.
- Pray daily for Salvationists compelled to join in the fighting, that they might be examples of faithfulness and lead many to seek salvation in Jesus.
- Pray for those sent out by the General to serve the bodies and souls of both sides.
- Pray that a holy revulsion against war will fill the hearts of all people everywhere.[6]

Notice the three cardinal principles in these directives ("guidance" is too weak a word to describe what Booth was giving to his people):

- Political neutrality
- Practical, compassionate outreach to the troops
- Soul winning among the troops.

The same three principles were enunciated when the First World War broke out in 1914, and again in the Second World War, 1939–1945. IHQ applied them with determination in each international crisis. The second and third principles are what anyone might expect of The Salvation Army. However, the first, that of *absolute political neutrality*, calls for close scrutiny of how it came to be seen as essential to a Salvationist stance and of whether it proved workable. It has already been noted that IHQ failed singularly to convince the territories that neutrality was an appropriate policy for the circumstances that prevailed in the World Wars when the moral issues at stake seemed clearer than in the 1899 conflict.

Significantly, within four weeks of the first article on war appearing in the London *War Cry*, it appeared word for word also in the South African *War Cry* with the explanation that the directives "apply equally to our South African comrades." This is truly pragmatic internationalism! The South Africa territorial commander, Commissioner George Kilbey, was obviously very comfortable with the approach and he announced to his people that he was a "World–Lover," loving both England and South Africa alike. In June 1900 he wrote in his *War Cry* column: "We Salvationists ... are under no obligation to have any opinion as to the righteousness or otherwise of the war. A pronouncement on its character is therefore not required from us. We are opposed to all strife everywhere."[7] More political neutrality. He was merely echoing the line taken in London at IHQ where in September 1899 the *War Cry* had declared that "if there is blame, it is shared by *both* sides." As to the causes and the issues?—"This is not our business!"[8]

William Booth's realism did not abandon him. He freely acknowledged that Salvationists would and could hold personal views on the war and even on the politics of it. But they were to keep these always to themselves. As Salvationists, there could be absolutely no taking of sides. All war was "of the devil," and so how could any saved person ever support it for any cause?[9] His motive was a pragmatic one. He was utterly determined that when the war ended, South Africa would still be part of the Salvation Army world. International ties were a sacred trust, and he, as General, was chief trustee.

The same pragmatic motivation caused him to offer no opinion to his people on the morality of carrying arms in time of war. Not once did he advocate that they should, and neither did he proclaim that they should not. He told them that this was a matter for the individual conscience of each Salvationist. Already there were numerous active Salvationists in the ranks of the fighting men. Was Booth to tell them their profession was unworthy? After all, there was New Testament precedent for their position. Booth intuited that to take an official position one way or the other would be deeply divisive. By making private conscience the arbiter, he avoided any split in his ranks on the issue, and the same position is that of the worldwide Army to this day. It should be noted that in the Boer War there was no conscription and that each side relied upon regular soldiers or volunteers. Later wars, of course, involved compulsory military service and the accompanying phenomenon of conscientious objection.

The War Cry for October 21, 1899 published the first article on war to carry Booth's own name. His heart was "torn asunder," and he felt "deepest humiliation and bitterest regrets" for mankind. Two nations had pushed aside reason, humanity and religion. Victory would go to the side that "can kill and wound the largest number of human beings and keep on the longest at the wretched business."[10] He wept for Salvationists fighting Salvationists, for the suffering, for widows and orphans yet to be and over the hindrances that would come to the Army's work in both lands. He was fearful lest "the passions that almost invariably track the dogs of war" should overtake Salvationists, for "delight in havoc and ruin" were not in accord with the spirit of Jesus Christ.[11] His words were picked up and reported in the secular press, with some approval.

A few months into the war, the Founder felt it necessary to announce a total prohibition on Salvationists taking part in "demonstrations, meetings, processions, or the like" if these were carried on "upon political or party lines."[12] A similar prohibition was to be promulgated in the two World Wars. By now Booth's tone was sterner, more autocratic than six months before. It seems the pulling power of patriotic fervor was taking its toll among his Salvationists, and there is evidence that Salvation Army buildings and Salvation Army bands were being used for some of the meetings and rallies with wartime political themes. He could not have turned a blind eye to this.

The stance of political neutrality was not kept under wraps as far as the general public was concerned. It was spelled out with force and clarity in the Army's main public relations periodical at that time, *All The World*.[13] Booth was ready to risk a negative reaction from his financial supporters, placing principle before income. At one stage, when a peace treaty appeared likely, Booth told the Army that there was to be no show of disrespect for the vanquished, no vindictive exultation, no ceremonies inconsistent with Army principles and no believing the worst about those on the other side, for instead Salvationists should be hoping the best for them. He told his Army: "Push your own war, the holy war, the war of love, the war of God."[14]

It was early in June 1902 that hostilities ended, and the *War Cry* attributed this to "the work of the Spirit of God."[15] It carried on its cover a depiction of the angel of peace hovering over an officer of The Salvation Army preaching to a British and a Boer soldier. Inside Booth exhorted his people in both Britain and South Africa to work for reconciliation. In the Transvaal over 6,000 Boers had perished, and at home the families of 20,000 British soldiers mourned their dead, while the loved ones of 70, 000 wounded men faced a highly uncertain future.[16]

It had all been an ordeal for the Army too, as leaders in London struggled to lift the horizons of Salvationists on both sides above narrow nationalism. Practical lessons emerged, however, as for the first time the Army entered into intensive ministry in a war zone with military personnel and with their families in both countries. The principal vehicle for Salvationist evangelism and practical service in the war was the Naval and Military League (NML).[17] Its motto was "Love Conquers All." Its aims: to get military personnel saved through their Salvationist colleagues; to keep those already saved true to God; and to render compassionate and practical service to meet the needs thrown up by a state of war. Only committed Salvationists could be members of the NML, which was perceived as an order within The Salvation Army. By the end of 1900 it was represented in 235 battalions and batteries of the British forces and on 131 ships of the British navy. Homes for soldiers and sailors had been established in 14 locations: four in England, two in the Mediterranean, one each in Japan and India and six in South Africa.[18] The strategy for human service outreach among the fighting men was simple—find out what they need most and provide it, if it is legal! Mother the troops in small, practical ways with clothing, letter writing, supplies of stationery, good inexpensive food, recreational facilities and round–the–clock visitation of their families. A Prayer Union for wives was formed, and a newsletter went out entitled "Under the Colors."

The First World War, 1914

Germany invaded Belgium on August 4, 1914. Again, war had

come. The London *War Cry* at once reprinted William Booth's first Boer War article, even though he had died in 1912. Only weeks before the onset of hostilities The Salvation Army had concluded its 1914 International Congress during which 4,000 delegates had gathered in London, England, from 58 countries and colonies to celebrate their God–given internationalism. The British press gave the event some prominence, but special attention focused on the 164 Salvationists who made up the contingent from Germany. The German Staff Band was featured in musical recitals.

This Congress was a thanksgiving for the 30 percent growth in Army work and witness between 1904 and 1914. The international Salvation Army looked something like this in 1914 as war befell the world:

- Working in 58 lands
- Using 35 languages
- Operating in 9,516 church (corps) centers
- Having 16,438 commissioned, ordained officers
- Employing 22,150 additional full–time staff
- Offering social service in 1,168 institutions.[19]

One year short of its fiftieth anniversary from the founding of The Christian Mission in 1865, the Army was solidly established in all the countries destined to play a large part in the war. Britain and America regarded the Army as part of the national fabric of life. The work in Belgium was supervised from France, where the work was hard but on a firm footing. Germany had 150 corps, 20 of them in Berlin alone, and a large force of officers numbering over 500. Some of these were British.[20]

For the second time in its short history, the Army's international bonds and network were to be severely tested, and Salvationists would once again fight on opposing sides in battle. Many of the public thought it would all be over by Christmas, and men flocked in large numbers to join up, eager to get to the heart of the action. But it was not to be. By 1916 the British government had introduced conscription, and war fever gripped the population. Everything

German became an object of hatred, so that even Dachshund dogs were stoned in the streets![21]

The Army's first thought was to rediscover the lessons of the 1899–1902 Boer War. From the start, the international *War Cry* in London struck the same note of supranational neutrality and idealism as it had throughout the Boer conflict. General Bramwell Booth, having succeeded his father in 1912, told his officers to put prayer first and to take no side: "As Salvationists, our nation, like our Master's, includes all nations."[22]

It has to be said that General Bramwell was not always able to keep his private views to himself. These revealed a strong desire for a British victory, but he kept consistently, even doggedly, to the official policy line of political neutrality in his public and printed pronouncements directed to Salvationists. His wife, Florence Booth, writing in the October 24, 1914 *War Cry*, gave her unabashed opinion: "Praying for victory is not an option open to Christians, since my victory must mean equally defeat for others."[23]

This was, of course, a highly contentious assertion. It was to find no favor in other Army territories either in this war or the next, but for now the wife of the second General was adamant that her readers should feel the force of her anti–war sentiments. It was all part of IHQ's determination to take no sides, and to let German Salvationists know and feel, rightly, they were still seen and wanted as part of the international Salvation Army. Keeping the Army intact, free from schism, and as united as ever was a sacred trust. The second General and his wife felt this as much as the first.

None of this, however, prevented the Army in the United Kingdom from going on to a war footing. All over the country, officers visited the families of men called to carry arms. Over 100 officers were posted to serve at military encampments. The Naval and Military Homes were offered to the government for their use. Several Army citadels (corps buildings) were commandeered for military use. Officers at headquarters offered to take field ap-pointments to fill the gaps left by those who had been transferred to the military bases, and all officers took a cut in their already meager allowances, volunteering to forego all leave for the duration of the war. Funds ran short; needs redoubled and redoubled again; buildings were taken over or destroyed; loyalties were strained; patriotism competed with an almost impossibly idealistic political neutrality; and all against a permanent backdrop of running battles with government departments over who could do what and where it could or could not be done!

It was a time of unprecedented difficulty. Bramwell Booth watched as money set aside for the deploying of 100 missionary officers was diverted to the war work. Key officers in Germany, France and Belgium were being forced to give military service. "Men are dead who were formerly so brave and splendid in their testimony to Christ. Some of our men we have lost in the struggle against ungodliness and worldliness," wrote the General. The ranks were growing thin. He blamed the government's policy of providing alcohol for the troops and licensed brothels in the war zones, "a sheer madness for which the nation will have to pay dear in generations to come."[24]

Salvationist efforts at even-handedness between the warring sides were given tangible embodiment in various ways. Army editors were told not to use the word "enemy" in any Army publication. Army writers tried to present German people and even German military personnel in a favorable and human light. An Ambulance Brigade was formed and publicly dedicated to the service of the wounded of *all* nations, something that worked out in actual practice. The London *War Cry* carried stories of grateful German soldiers helped by Salvationists.[25] The bandages made from the "Old Linen Campaign" in the United States before Americans entered the war were sent for use by Germans as well as the allies of Britain.[26] Ministry was carried out to German civilian internees and to German prisoners of war all over Europe.

Captain Carvosso Gauntlett, later the IHQ Editor in Chief during the Second World War and a deeply convinced pacifist, led the way, visiting every internment camp in England, Scotland and Wales, as well as on the Isle of Man off the west coast of England where new communities of German internees sprang up numbering between 3,000 and 20,000 persons. Gauntlett was also in charge of

Salvationist ministry to German prisoners of war, travelling more than 17,000 miles each year and visiting over 50,000 prisoners.[27] Army officers in occupied Belgium adopted the same spirit toward the German troops there. Bramwell Booth, whenever news reached him of any Salvationist helping a member of the fighting forces of a hostile country, ensured the story was given a high profile in the Army press. He also gave publicity in the international *War Cry* to the witness carried on by German Salvation Army officers who had been conscripted into the German army.[28]

Inside Germany, expulsion orders were issued against all expatriate Army personnel.[29] Links with IHQ were severed. Little official information flowed to the London center, and the *Year Book* for all the war years shows the same statistics for Germany for each year of the war as those published in 1914.[30] Six corps of the 20 in Berlin were closed down. Work very similar to that conducted in the rest of Europe for the fighting troops was begun, including a letter exchange for lonely men at the front, the conversion of the Officer Training College in Berlin into an Industrial Center for released prison inmates and a migration scheme for children that took 45,000 German children to safety in Hungary. German Salvationists removed the British "S" from their uniforms and replaced it with the German "H" for "Heilsarmee." By the end of the war, 20 officers had been killed on active service, and many more non–officer Salvationists with them.[31]

All this shows that political neutrality and an even–handed approach was both possible and pragmatic, but the question remains as to whether or not this was the *only* way to protect the Army's internationalism, and whether or not it was *morally* acceptable to see internationalism only in terms of neutrality.

Evangeline Booth's American Army

The United States remained officially neutral in the war until April 1917, but The Salvation Army there began to react sooner. Bramwell Booth's sister, Evangeline, was in charge of the Army in the States. Late in 1914 she joined the World's Peace Committee, launched a drive for funds to assist Belgian refugees and laid down plans to form the Naval and Military League in America. By January 1915 Eva had successfully embarked upon her "Old Linen Campaign," which produced 400,000 packages of sterilized bandages sent to all protagonists in Europe. This effort also provided employment for 300 American women.[32]

As soon as the United States entered the war (technically to protect neutral rights to international sea lanes), patriotic feeling swept through the country, carrying American Salvationists with it. This was unremarkable and entirely reasonable. The only factor that raised a question mark over it was the IHQ policy of strict political neutrality. Perhaps the international center could manage this, but to ask it of an Army whose life was lived with its roots going deep into the soil of American patriotism and nation–building was altogether unrealistic.

One headquarters officer, Alexander Damon, recorded in his diary: "Fever to enlist is running high on our building. Many of the young fellows feel they must go ... Some who are officers decline to claim exemption even if they could."[33] Evangeline Booth publicly threw her Army behind the American government. In her first public article after the entry into the war, she eulogized President Woodrow Wilson for his "superb magnanimity" toward Germany and his "phenomenal patience." He had displayed "the greatest executive genius," and now had the "united spirit of a free people" behind him. Eva announced that the Army's hatred of war would not prevent Salvationists standing by the President "to the last man," and ended by pledging the loyalty of every Salvationist to the American cause and urging her people not to fail their country.[34] No political neutrality here! After April 1917 the American *War Cry* dropped all mention of Germans or The Salvation Army in Germany.

A War Service League was organized for, as Eva put it, the civilian counterpart of activity at the front. The drive for memberships was based explicitly upon the need to defeat Germany. Her appeals for funds for the Army were to help the Army help America to win the war. The divergence from the London stance could not have been more stark. Eva saw her Army as part of the American war machine and did not hesitate to say so.

In 1919 she published her account of Salvationist war work, *The War Romance of The Salvation Army.* This was ghost–written for her by Grace Livingstone Hill as a fund–raising tool. It proved a great success, but at the price of referring to Germans as "Huns," "Fritzy" and "the Boche" throughout.[35] It gave the impression that American Salvationists were indeed the sworn enemies of the German people. She came under sharp criticism from other members of her family circle for the tone adopted in the book. But Eva's determination and leadership skills could not be faulted. She rallied the Army in the United States as never before and went on to fashion an impressive and effective multi–faceted program of wartime work both at home and in the theatre of operations where American troops were to be found.

It was here that the first Army "doughnut" was baked.[36] It was produced for members of the American Expeditionary Force in Europe. Having run short of rations, and faced with hungry soldiers, female officers at the front wondered what to give them. Margaret Sheldon hit upon the idea of doughnuts, and Helen Purviance is reputed to have made the first one.[37] The Army did not look back after that inspired culinary expedient!

Over 80,000 American Salvationists and clients in the care of the Salvation Army were drafted for military service, but the Army girls won the hearts of all the fighting men.[38] As in Britain, they sought simply to mother them, and it worked. In her *War Romance,* Eva said the success was due to three things:

- The Army's preparedness
- Its familiarity with hardship
- Its practical religion, reducing theory to action and revealing Christ in deeds.[39]

When the war ended, Eva launched a Home Service Fund, and a grateful American public gave $15 million, $2 million in excess of her target.[40] Salvation Army service to Americans caught up in the strife won for the Army in the United States a lasting place of deep affection in the hearts of all her citizens, even if more than one "politically neutral" eyebrow had been raised at IHQ.

Divergence Elsewhere

It was not only in America that the IHQ policy of political neutrality failed to take hold. In Australia the territorial commander, Commissioner James Hay, was delighted when he heard that a warship had been named "USS Salvation Lass" and called it a gracious gesture on the part of the authorities. IHQ remained silent, sensing no doubt that if you were supposed to be politically neutral, it did not do to have warships named after you. Commissioner Hay's reactions to the outbreak of war were simple and direct—it was a fight for right and civilization against barbarism. No neutrality on either the politics or the ethical issues. He saw the Army as "the British Empire's 'Salvation Ally'" and the war as a "gallant stand for God and the Empire." In his Armistice address on November 12, 1918, Hay flatly told his audience that the defeat of Germany was the work of God.[41] At IHQ they felt the same, but were not willing to say so in any official public utterance or publication.

The Australian Salvationists' response in the war can be seen personified in William McKenzie, a legendary figure nicknamed "Fighting Mac." He was the first Australian military chaplain, a winner of the Military Cross, and his name became a household word. His battle–field exploits became widely known, and the Australian *War Cry* gave them great prominence.[42] This drew from General Bramwell Booth at IHQ a forthright rebuke for the territorial commander, reminding him that officers were not to take on combatant roles (McKenzie had taken over command of his unit on the battlefield when all the military officers were shot down) and that the Army was not to "get caught up in the worldly aspect of the war."[43]

Hay was told in plain language to "beware of it. Keep in mind that you are international—as Jesus Christ was ... we must hold up the great principles of love and universal brotherhood ... a word to the wise is sufficient."[44] All the available evidence indicates that Bramwell's message was ineffective in influencing the openness of the outright patriotism and partisanship of Australian Salvationists at all levels. When McKenzie came home, his public welcome meeting in Melbourne drew 7,000 people, and another 1,000 were turned away.

Attitudes in New Zealand were the same as those found in Australia. It was not realistic to expect anything else. New Zealand was the first Empire country to appoint Salvation Army officers as military chaplains, and throughout the hostilities Salvationists there identified entirely with the cause for which their own kith and kin were fighting, even though war itself was seen as evil but sometimes unavoidable. The territory's official report on their war work, an unpublished document held in the Army's New Zealand archives, summarized things by saying openly that Germany started the war, and that "the Salvation Army flag followed the Union Jack."[45] This was true, but it was not the whole truth, for Salvationists were ministering to the troops and civilian populations of all the warring nations. However, from a New Zealand perspective, it was what the Army there saw and did.

Political neutrality failed also in India. The allied military authorities in the Persian Gulf asked The Salvation Army in India to raise two regiments of "porter coolies." According to the New Zealand territory's war work report, the Army said they would (IHQ policy not withstanding), and two non–combatant regiments, each of 600 men, left India for Mesopotamia, where they were known as "The Salvation Army Porter Coolie Corps." They were used to load and offload ships in the Gulf, and were under the command of three British Salvation Army officers holding the military rank of Second–Lieutenant, assisted by two Indian Salvation Army officers.[46] IHQ could not possibly have been unaware of this arrangement. It is interesting to note that not one single word about it ever appeared in any official Army publication anywhere in the world. It cut right across any policy of neutrality.

1939: World Conflict Again!

Germany, under Adolf Hitler, invaded Poland. To honor her treaty obligations, Britain declared war on Germany on September 3, 1939. At once The Salvation Army in the United Kingdom was

again put on a war footing. By now Evangeline Booth was the
General, but was soon to retire. A High Council had convened and
had elected George L. Carpenter to succeed her. He was a pacifist.
He held office throughout the war years, including an extension to
his tenure well into 1946 due to the impracticality of convening
another High Council in war conditions. The Army's global statistics
at the end of the fighting were as follows:

- Ministry to 225,000,000 troops
- Establishment of 3,000 Red Shield Clubs for military personnel
- 595,000 wounded persons and their families visited and given practical help
- 1,000 mobile canteens in operation, each serving
  4,600 men per trip
- These mobile canteens covered a distance during
  the war equivalent to four times round the
  world.[47]

This third wartime ordeal by fire for Salvationist internationalism was the worst one of all. Precious bonds with fellow
Salvationists that had been built up over years, or which had been
lovingly restored after 1918, were to be torn asunder in the maelstrom of a war that would engulf the world and inflict suffering on
a scale no one had ever experienced or even thought possible.
Leaders at IHQ once again made internationalism their watchword.
No official or formal statement or comment was to emerge from
IHQ during the war years that put blame upon Hitler or Nazism for
the plight of the nations. The stance of political neutrality, which
was by now time–honored, began to look like moral neutrality too.
No thought was given to the possibility that the cardinal principal
of neutrality, which William Booth had pushed for when the Boer
War began in 1899, was not meant to work as a gag for the
international Salvation Army in a conflict on an altogether different
and global scale and in which there were ethical issues begging for
a Salvationist voice to be heard. The neutrality policy for which

IHQ again opted left the Army's world center silent on the sheer evil and wrongness of Hitler's aggression. Instead, there were anguished pronouncements about the abhorrent nature of war in general. Once again it fell to the territories to be specific and outspoken about the rights and wrongs of *this* war.

Internationalism and Nazi Germany

The 1914–1918 war had decimated the Salvation Army in Germany by at least 40 percent of its strength. Hitler refrained from action against the Army in the early and mid 1930s, even though other churches experienced persecution. On December 8, 1934 the Gestapo in Berlin issued a directive that no action should be taken against The Salvation Army because it was not a political movement and also because of the effect upon relations with Britain.[48] All able–bodied men were forced to enlist. There was no such thing as conscientious objection. You joined the forces or you were shot. Slowly restrictions were imposed that cut off the Army's income, so that the older and the female officers had to take secular work in order to raise funds simply to eat. Hitler outlawed the German *War Cry*. Contact with IHQ ended, although occasional news filtered through via neutral Sweden. While Army street marches were still allowed, they had to be headed by a flag bearing the Swastika Cross. Hermann Goring gave gifts of toys at Christmas to Army children's homes, but disbanded the Girl Guides. All youth activities fell under state control. Then the burning of Bibles began, including those of the Army. Public fund raising was prohibited, the use of military ranks was stopped, and no Salvationist could be referred to as a "soldier." Next, all Army property was expropriated by the state, but many of the local authorities asked Army personnel to continue to run the buildings as there were no other staff to take over!

Ironically, the real physical devastation came not from within Germany, but from without. On the night of February 2, 1945, 1,000 Allied aircraft bombed Berlin, and among the buildings destroyed was the territorial headquarters and all the officers' accommodation next to it. When Berlin eventually fell, Russian troops stabled their horses in the basement of the ruins. All in all,

33 out of 88 Army church buildings were totally destroyed and six others seriously damaged. Of the 34 social centers, 13 were lost and five badly damaged. One building lost was a maternity hospital equipped with more than 100 beds. Allied bombs killed the matron, Captain Ilse Handel. Over 200 Salvationists were killed either in battle or in the air raids.[49] In 1946, General Albert Orsborn, Carpenter's successor, visited Berlin and wrote of it in his auto-biography: "I just looked and wept ... It was a charnel–house ... all naked horror."[50]

Pearl Harbor

December 7, 1941 is a date indelibly etched upon the American psyche. It was a sunny Sunday morning and the date of the attack upon Pearl Harbor. It was also the end of America's neutrality. Wave after wave of Japanese planes swept over the American Pacific Fleet. The fleet, the airfields and the surrounding troops were all caught off guard. Before long the fleet was incapacitated. The local Salvation Army swung into action in the Schofield Barracks where Major and Mrs. Alva M. Holbrook were in charge. Mrs. Holbrook produced more than 4,000 doughnuts in 24 hours.[51]

There were five Army corps and four social institutions on the island of Oahu, Hawaii, and almost at once local families were seeking shelter. On the night of December 7, 100 families were cared for at the institution at Manoa, and another 100 in the gymnasium of the Boys' Home at Kaimuki. A temporary food station was set up for civilian men who worked at Pearl Harbor. Two Army officers stationed themselves on either side of the street leading from Pearl Harbor, and as the men trailed homeward after work, they were each asked if they had eaten. On the first night, 127 men were fed. Members of the police force also ate at the Army until more permanent arrangements could be made. Salvationist personnel visited the homes of more than 1,000 Japanese residents in the downtown area in the first week after the attack. This was especially significant. The Girls' Home in Upper Manila was designated as the receiving station for lost children as well as distraught or sick women. A Red Cross surgical dressing center was set up. It employed women of every nationality on the island and made over 500,000 surgical dressings during the war.[52]

By the 1940s The Salvation Army in the United States was organized on the basis of a National Headquarters and four territories, each producing its own *War Cry*. The main theme of articles written in the aftermath of the attack on the fleet was that America had now been forced into war. Any neutral tone that had prevailed earlier disappeared overnight. All the Army's top leaders announced that The Salvation Army was behind the government for victory, just as Evangeline Booth had done in the last war. There was to be no attempt at internationalist idealism. The record of American Salvation Army war work after Pearl Harbor and through the remaining years of conflict is truly one of expert organizational skills, swift and relevant responses to war needs and an aligning with the national effort that left the whole of America in not the slightest doubt that The Salvation Army was out to win the war.

The Neutrality Policy

The carrying on of intensive soul–winning activities and of social service work in the war were simply instinctive reactions of a true Salvationist heartbeat adapted to war conditions. It was the third component of the official IHQ Salvationist stance, that of political neutrality, which marks the Army wartime attitude as unique among all the churches. No other Christian organization attempted such a combination of policies:

- Evangelism: getting the troops saved
- Compassionate Action: meeting every conceivable variety of human need thrown up by the war and doing so with high skill and pragmatism
- Political (and Moral?) Neutrality: staying high above the war spirit that swept the participating populations, refusing to comment on the causes, conduct or any of the moral issues that arose in the three wars, and even on the morality or otherwise of Nazism and its practices, so that there

never has been an official Salvation Army statement from IHQ saying that Nazism was evil.

These three principles composed the official policy at the
international center, because it was thought that the Army's
internationalist ethos necessitated such a stance. The historical
source materials for all three wars give no hint that serious
consideration was ever given to whether or not it would have been
possible to continue to bear witness to an internationalist ideal
and yet adopt some line of policy other than that of being politically
neutral. How can you be neutral when the world is menaced by a
criminal megalomaniac? Neutrality does nothing to restrain the
evildoer. Nevertheless, it was seen by leaders at IHQ as the only
available option for an international community in time of war. Its
goal was to keep the worldwide Army intact and to give embodiment
to the internationalist ethos that was precious to all parts of the
Army world.

All three Generals believed that the international Army was a
sacred trust from God, and that without its international dimensions
and loyalties the Army could no longer be the Army as God intended
it to be. The most compelling need, therefore, and the overriding
priority was the avoidance of a split in the international ranks.
Nothing was to be said, done or written that might threaten schism
or alienate any part of the Army. All the Generals perceived this as
their duty.

Apart from the occasional mention of various well–known Bible
passages (such as 1 Corinthians 12–13; Galatians 3:28; Ephesians
4:4–6), the neutralist policy was never given any clearly articulated
underlying rationale. IHQ offered little by way of philosophical or
theological justification for it, being content with the New
Testament references. In the absence of a compelling rationale, the
simple fact that the Army stood alone among the churches in its
neutrality raises acutely the question of whether or not the IHQ
policy was in error. Put another way: was Evangeline Booth right
and were the three wartime Generals wrong?

Exactly what principle gave birth to a policy of political and moral neutrality? Why was it seen as so inappropriate for the Salvation Army to pass a moral judgment on the behavior of the warring factions? For example, did the Army claim some distinctive vocation under God and within the universal body of Christ on earth to dissociate altogether from politics? If so, neutrality could have been seen as an obedient response to that vocation. But no such vocation was, or has subsequently been, claimed either for the Army organizationally or for Salvationists individually.

From its earliest days the Army has involved itself in the political process. It has always acted in a non–partisan role, but has passed judgment upon government policies and their impact upon the Army's traditional constituency, the poorest of the poor. It has to be concluded that what IHQ was willing to do in peacetime in relation to domestic politics, it was unwilling to do in relation to inter–nation politics in wartime. There never was a reasoned attempt to justify or explain this shift from one approach to the other. In fact, in all the millions of words written and in all the hundreds of publications printed by the Army in the three wars there is not even the slightest hint that this anomaly was ever noticed by Salvationists. There seems only to have been an automatic assumption that Salvationist internationalism necessitated Salvationist political and moral neutrality as an official IHQ policy.

This policy was simply announced by William Booth in 1899, copied by Bramwell Booth in 1914 and stated again by George Carpenter in 1939. The absence of any challenge to, or questioning of, the policy at IHQ points to the immensely strong and lasting influence of William Booth on his successors in office and upon later generations of Salvationists. Did he see himself as legislating the Army's response in all wars for all time? Or would he not have expected his successors to think for themselves in the changed circumstances of later conflicts? Neutrality suited his purpose in 1899, but it is hard to imagine William Booth, had he been alive in 1939, not coming out clearly against National Socialism in Germany and doing it in such a way that left German Salvationists in no doubt that they were, nevertheless, loved and wanted as part of the worldwide Army. He could never have remained silent on the evils of Nazism or the rightness of opposing it and its organizers by all available means.

One final question presents itself: whether the fears that led to the neutrality policy would have been realized if that policy had not been followed. These fears were basically threefold:

- The fear that outspokenness by IHQ against a warring state or its leaders would lead to the persecution of Salvationists (for example, in Germany, Italy or Japan)
- The fear that outspokenness would result in the proscription of The Salvation Army in countries opposed to Britain in the wars
- The fear that taking moral or political sides would produce schism in the international Army, so that for instance the Italian or German or Japanese Salvationists might move to secede from the international Army, rejecting the authority of IHQ and of the General.

Persecution of Salvationists, merely because they were Salvationists, was virtually unknown in any of the three wars. Nothing happened to compare, for example, with Hitler's treatment of the Jehovah's Witnesses, whose beliefs led them to refuse military service and who were all shot.[53] Individual Salvationists encountered personal suffering in the wars, but this was not directly attributable to their Salvationism. We simply cannot say today whether the giving of a clearer moral lead at IHQ would have led to persecution of Salvationists for their Salvationism. Some have suggested that the Army should have sided overtly with the righteous cause regardless of the costs. That is an easy judgment to make from the comfort of the present day. Matters were not so clear cut to those in life or death peril years ago.

The fear of being outlawed was in fact realized. Heavy restrictions were imposed on the Army, especially in the Second World War, and a policy of neutrality was helpless to prevent it.

The fear that the Army would be split was not realized. However, there is a strong case to be made that schism could in any event have been avoided even if IHQ had abandoned neutrality. Other churches made no secret of their opposition to Nazism both before and during the war, yet were not taken to be turning their backs on fellow Christians in Germany. By careful preparation, using the Swedish connection with German Salvationists in the Second World War, London could have forged appropriate attitudes at an official level and expressed them in terms which left Salvationists in Germany sensing plainly that any condemnation of German policy was not to be taken as distancing the international Army from local German Salvationists. Such an approach would have been a simple extension of the Army's often–repeated statement that the wars were not wars between the masses of the people, but wars between their governments.

As it was, no prophetic Salvationist voice was heard raised at IHQ addressing in a specific and relevant way events that were traumatizing people, including Salvationists, everywhere. Army leaders played it safe, thereby unintentionally creating the impression that the Army was not only politically neutral, but was morally neutral too. In striking contrast to the territories, such as in the United States, where the Army's response to the outbreak of war was spontaneously partisan and uninhibited, the international center inadvertently allowed itself to be perceived as though disinclined to wrestle with the real ethical issues, and as perhaps complacent concerning a truly deep involvement with a world at war. It settled for old policies in new situations.

All the splendid intensity of soul–saving efforts in the wars and all the burning energy poured out all over the world in devotion to practical human need, do not, in retrospect, hide the ultimate inadequacy of the neutrality thought by IHQ leaders to be an inescapable consequence of Salvationist internationalism. It became indeed their "crown of thorns."[54]

A Century Beckons

When the twenty–first century dawns, The Salvation Army will enter the third century on which it has been invited to leave its mark. Conversely, that century will also make its mark on the Army, as it should. Genuine interaction with the age in which we live is a two–way process. This demands that a church should have the capacity to face anything that comes along and retain its poise, for its roots are in Christ who is the same yesterday, today and forever.

As the year 1900 dawned, few could have predicted what the twentieth century would bring: two world wars; weapons so destructive that the human race can now destroy itself and its planet many, many times over; the rise and fall of communism; emancipation of women in large parts of the world; the divorce deluge; the contraceptive pill; the spread of compulsory education for children; unlocking of the secrets of flight; travel to the moon; exploration by unmanned craft beyond our solar system; new wealth; new poverty; political correctness; eradication of some dreadful diseases; onset of new diseases; a phenomenon some call homosexual marriage; the ongoing evangelization of the world; the re–emergence of militant, fundamentalist Islam; establishment of the community of nations; the never–ceasing presence of war; international terrorist networks; the coming of mass global communications systems through television and the computer; the information superhighway; globalization of pornography; wider sexual exploitation of children; pedophile tourist trips; entrenchment of child labor; the phenomenon of atheist priests and heretical bishops in the church; struggle for church unity; the biological revolution with its impersonal procreation techniques; widespread acceptability of social convenience abortions, with its culture of death; easy disposal of the fatally ill; global warming; potentially disastrous climate changes; eradication of countless animal species ...

The list could be expanded almost endlessly. Some of it is good; much of it is bad. Sin thrives. The world is sick.

The next century will bring more of the same, and worse. Yet Jesus is the same.[1] How shall we respond? What can we do? Is there anything new to try? What can we say, that we have not said before? What will they write about us at the end of the twenty–first century? We do not know, and we do not need to know. The veiling of the future is one way in which our loving Creator protects us. However, we are allowed to hope.

We can hope that someone somewhere will judge that The Salvation Army got it right because it proved itself highly and swiftly adaptable to changing times, without betraying its roots or vocation. We can hope they will say that this Protestant, evangelical, pragmatic and international church, with its distinctive, intuitive sacramentalism, and with its highly charged social conscience, was not thrown off balance by a twenty–first century of bewildering, and frighteningly rapid, social and technological change. We can hope they will record that we retained, and where needful rediscovered, our passion—and giftedness—for introducing people to Jesus Christ as Lord and Savior, and that we led daring–to–be–different, sanctified lives of sacrificial service to others. We can hope too that the historians will not accuse us of settling for stale policies in fresh situations. We must also hope they will write about the new energy and dynamism that surged into the Army from its new converts—people of all backgrounds, all races and all ages. Will they say about us, 100 years from now, that the Army stayed alive and relevant, true to its divine calling, because in the twenty–first century it demonstrated holy nerve and courage, trusting in God's promise to do a daring, new thing?[2]

I grant the closing words of this analysis to an officer of The Salvation Army who retired in the twentieth century, but even yet strains to catch a glimpse of the century that beckons. Old and seasoned now, but still spirited, he wrote to me reflecting upon a lifetime of service and ministry. His letter came as these final pages were being drafted. In it he wrote: "No regrets—only that I wish I'd had more faith, more daring."

Jesus, Jesus, Lord of the future, come and help us now.

APPENDIX A

The Doctrines of The Salvation Army

We believe that the Scriptures of the Old and New Testaments were given by inspiration of God, and that they only constitute the divine rule of Christian faith and practice.

We believe that there is only one God, who is infinitely perfect, the Creator, Preserver and Governor of all things, and who is the only proper object of religious worship.

We believe that there are three persons in the Godhead—the Father, the Son and the Holy Ghost, undivided in essence and co–equal in power and glory.

We believe that in the person of Jesus Christ the Divine and human natures are united, so that He is truly and properly God and truly and properly man.

We believe that our first parents were created in a state of innocency, but by their disobedience they lost their purity and happiness, and that in consequence of their fall all men have become sinners, totally depraved, and as such are justly exposed to the wrath of God.

We believe that the Lord Jesus Christ has by His suffering and death made an atonement for the whole world so that whosoever will may be saved.

We believe that repentance towards God, faith in our Lord Jesus Christ, and regeneration by the Holy Spirit, are necessary to salvation.

We believe that we are justified by grace through faith in our Lord Jesus Christ and that he that believeth hath the witness in himself.

We believe that continuance in a state of salvation depends upon continued obedient faith in Christ.

We believe that it is the privilege of all believers to be wholly sanctified, and that their whole spirit, soul and body may be preserved blameless unto the coming of our Lord Jesus Christ.

We believe in the immortality of the soul; in the resurrection of the body; in the general judgment at the end of the world; in the eternal happiness of the righteous; and in the endless punishment of the wicked.

APPENDIX B

Salvation Army National Memberships in Ecumenical and Interchurch Bodies

American Bible Society
American Camping Association
    Council of Religiously Affiliated Camps
American Society on Aging
    Forum on Religion, Spirituality and Aging
Association of Evangelical Relief and Development Organizations
Association of Statisticians of American Religious Bodies
Billy Graham Center Institute for Prison Ministries
Christian Camping Association
    National Executive Group
Christian Holiness Partnership
Christian Legal Society
Christian Management Association
Christian Stewardship Association
Christians for Biblical Equality
    Sexual Abuse National Task Force
Commission for Church and Youth Agency Relations
Concerts of Prayer International
Denominational Executives of Christian Education
Evangelical Press Association
Evangelicals for Social Action
International Christian Education Association
InterVarsity Christian Fellowship
    Student Mission Convention
Lausanne Committee for World Evangelization
Laymen's National Bible Association
Mission America
    AD 2000 and Beyond Movement
    AD 2000 Women's Track
Mission Literature Society

National Association of Christians in Social Work
National Association of Evangelicals
National Black Evangelical Association
National Day of Prayer Task Force
National Interfaith Cable Coalition
National Prayer Committee
North American Association of Christians in Social Work
North American Conference of Church Men's Staff
North American Society for Church Growth
Promise Keepers
Religion in American Life
Religious Conference Management Association
Religious Alliance Against Pornography
Religious Public Relations Council
United States Church Leaders
Walk Through the Bible Ministries
Wesleyan/Holiness Women's Clergy

Notes

Chapter 1

1. John Coutts, *The Salvationists* (London: Mowbrays, 1977), 21.

2. Catherine Booth, *The Salvation Army in Relation to the Church and State, And Other Addresses* (London: The Salvation Army, 1889).

3. Galatians 6:10; 2 Corinthians 11:2.

4. Frederick Coutts, *The Salvation Army in Relation to the Church* (London: Salvationist Publishing and Supplies Ltd., 1977), 7.

5. William J. Cozens, *Annual Report of The Salvation Army, Inc. in Boston, MA: The Church of the Back Street* (Boston: The Salvation Army, 1900).

6. *Definitive Statement of Salvation Army Services and Activities in the USA* (New York: The Salvation Army, 1989), 7 and 3.

7. *The Role of the Corps Officer in the USA: Guidelines for Corps Officers in the USA* (New York: The Salvation Army, 1972), 3 and 7.

8. *Southern Spirit* (Atlanta: The Salvation Army USA Southern Territory, September 24, 1998).

9. *Salvation Story: Salvationist Handbook of Doctrine* (London: Salvationist Publishing and Supplies Ltd., 1998), 100.

10. See Appendix A.

11. Lt. Colonel H. L. Taylor, ed., *Extracts From General Booth's Journal 1921–22* (London: Salvationist Publishing and Supplies Ltd., 1925), 30.

12. *Salvationist* (London: The Salvation Army United Kingdom Territory, June 20, 1998).

13. See Appendix B for a list of the 40 ecumenical and interchurch bodies in the United States of which the Army is an active member at the national level.

14. Judge Advocate General's Decision, September 12, 1917, U. S. War Department, Washington, D.C. (Judge G. T. Ansell, presiding).

15. The statutes were the provisions of the USA New Army Act in force on May 18, 1917.

Chapter 2

1. *The 1993 Directory For Ecumenism* (Washington, D.C.: Catholic News Service Documentary Service, 1993).

2. Brother Jeffrey Gros, "Protestants in the American Christian Community," *The Catholic World* (November/December 1995), 245.

3. *Catechism of the Catholic Church* (Liguori, USA: Liguori Publications, 1994), 222.

4. M. L. A. Cozens, *A Handbook of Heresies* (London: Sheed and Ward, 1979), v and 67.

5. Gros, 246–247.

6. See Appendix A.

7. *The Song Book of The Salvation Army, American Edition* (Verona, NJ: The Salvation Army National Headquarters, 1987). Hereafter cited as *SASB*.

8. See Appendix A.

9. *Salvation Story*, 1.

10. Ibid., 5.

11. See Appendix A.

12. Shaw Clifton, *Never the Same Again* (Alexandria: Crest Books, 1997). See chapters 6–8.

13. John 4:24.

Chapter 3

1. Mark A. Noll et al., *Evangelicalism: Comparative Studies of Popular Protestantism in North America, the British Isles, and Beyond* (Oxford: Oxford University Press, 1994).

2. Ibid., 5.

3. Richard J. Mouw, "Evangelicals and Catholics in Dialogue," *The Catholic World* (November/December 1995), 259–264.

4. See John 13:34–35.

5. Francis Schaeffer, *The God Who Is There* (Leicester: Inter–Varsity Press, 1990).

6. Michael Hamilton, "The Dissatisfaction of Francis Schaeffer," *Christianity Today* (March 3, 1997), 22–30.

7. Roger J. Green, *Catherine Booth: A Biography of the Co–founder of The Salvation Army* (Grand Rapids: Baker Books, 1996), 61.

8. See Appendix A.

9. *Salvationist*, 11.

10. News Release. International Headquarters, October 1998.

11. *Salvationist*, 4.

Chapter 4

1. William Booth, "The General's New Year Address To Officers," *The War Cry* (London: The Salvation Army International Headquarters, January 17, 1883), 4. Hereafter cited as *UKWC*.

2. William Booth, "Notes of The Majors' Councils," *UKWC*, November

4, 1882, 3.

3. Minnie Lindsay Carpenter, *Salvationists and the Sacraments* (London: Salvationist Publishing and Supplies Ltd., 1945), 5.

4. Ibid.

5. William Metcalf, *The Salvationist and the Sacraments* (London: Salvationist Publishing and Supplies Ltd., 1965), 24, 50–52.

6. Clifford Kew, *Closer Communion* (London: Salvationist Publishing and Supplies Ltd., 1980).

7. Paul A. Rader, "The Army's Position on the Sacraments" (San Pedro, CA: The Salvation Army USA Western Territory's Hispanic Ministries Seminar, May 9, 1994).

8. Ibid.; John 6:35.

9. Rader.

10. See Appendix A.

11. *The Book of Common Prayer* (London: Cambridge University Press, 1962), 294.

12. *Catechism*, 276.

13. Ibid., 289–291.

14. Ibid., Part Two, Section Two.

15. Ibid., 351–353.

16. See Appendix A.

17. *SASB*, 142, Song 512.

18. M. Basil Pennington, *Thomas Merton, Brother Monk: The Quest for True Freedom* (San Francisco: Harper & Row, 1987).

Chapter 5

1. Roger J. Green, from discussion at the meeting of the International Spiritual Life Commission, International College for Officers, London, March 21–27, 1997.

2. *UKWC*, January 17, 1883, 4.

3. *SASB*, 298, Song 993, verse 1.

4. Shaw Clifton, "Pakistan Territory Annual Report for 1998" (Lahore: The Salvation Army Pakistan Territorial Headquarters, February 1999).

5. Rader.

6. Samual Logan Brengle, *Love Slaves* (Atlanta: The Salvation Army, 1923, reprint 1982), 68–69.

7. John D. Waldron, *The Privilege of All Believers* (Atlanta: The Salvation Army, 1987), 114.

8. Ibid.

Chapter 6

1. *Salvationist*, 3.

2. Bishop John Austin Baker, letter to Lt. Colonel Robert Street, March 25, 1997.

3. Bishop John Austin Baker, "Sacraments," paper read at the meeting of the International Spiritual Life Commission, International College for Officers, London, March 24, 1997.

4. *Catechism*, 321, para. 1261, para. 1260.

5. Baker, "Sacraments."

6. Ibid.

7. "Move Forward in Freedom: International Spiritual Life Commission Report," *New Frontier* (Rancho Palos Verdes, CA: The Salvation Army USA Western Territory, May 7, 1998). For perceptive observations on the Love Feast based on long, practical experience, see Ed Read, *Jottings from My Journey* (Toronto: The Salvation Army, 1998), 217–219.

8. See 1 Corinthians 11:20–34.

9. "Love Feasts," *The Officer* (London: The Salvation Army, September 1895), 268.

10. "Move Forward."

11. Ibid.

12. Ibid.

13. See also *Called to Be God's People* (London: The Salvation Army International Headquarters, June 1998), a discussion booklet and aid for corps to look together at the International Spiritual Life Commission's "Call to Salvationists."

Chapter 7

1. See Genesis 3:1–20.

2. See Luke 4.

3. Genesis 3:1, 3, 4, 6.

4. See Appendix A.

5. Romans 3:10.

6. Romans 3:23.

7. Matthew 5:7.

8. Matthew 9:10; 2 Corinthians 5:21. See also Galatians 3:13 and 1 Peter 2:24.

9. Romans 3:23.

10. For example, *King James Version*: Galatians 1:16; 2:16, 20; 5:17. See also Ephesians 2:3 and Philippians 3:3.

11. Galatians 5:17, *New English Bible*.

12. Galatians 5:13, *Good News Bible*.

13. Galatians 5:19.

14. Romans 7:11.

15. C. K. Barrett, *Freedom and Obligation: A Study of the Epistle to the Galatians* (London: S.P.C.K., 1985), 75.

16. Galatians 5:19–21.

17. Galatians 5:21.

18. Galatians 5:22–23.

19. Clifton, *Never the Same Again.* See chapter 5.

20. Galatians 5:17.

21. Romans 8:1–13.

22. Clifton, *Never the Same Again.* See chapters 6–8.

23. *SASB*, 79, Song 286.

24. Ibid., 117, Song 416.

25. William Booth, "Holiness," *The Christian Mission Magazine* (London: The Christian Mission, August 1877), 193–198.

26. Ibid., 193.

27. Ibid., 193–195.

28. *SASB,* Song 416.

29. Booth, "Holiness," 196–197.

30. Ibid., 198.

31. Ibid., 200.

Chapter 8

1. *UKWC,* November 16, 1889, 10. This was a heading covering three local reports on a campaign to win 100,000 souls in six months. The same exhortation appeared on the first page of each edition of *The Officer* magazine, January 1898–January 1906.

2. *The Officers' Review* (London: The Salvation Army International Headquarters, January 1942), 33.

3. Barna Research Group, "What Effective Churches Have Discovered" 1996.

4. Robert E. Quinn, *Deep Change: Discovering the Leader Within* (San Francisco: Josey–Bass Publishers, 1996), chapter 20, p. 189.

5. A. P. Donajgrodzki, ed., *Social Control in Nineteenth Century Britain* (Totowa, NJ: Rowman and Littlefield, 1977), chapter 9.

6. Ibid., 237–241.

7. Ibid.

8. William Booth, *In Darkest England and the Way Out* (London: The Salvation Army, 1890), 17.

9. *SASB,* 191, Song 696, chorus.

10. Donajgrodzki, 237.

11. Ibid., 233–235.

12. Ibid., 242.

13. *Beatty v. Gillbanks* (1882). 15 Cox Criminal Cases (London). 9 Queen's Bench Division 308, 51 LJMC 117, 47 LT 194, 46 JP 789, Queen's Bench Divisional Court, England.

14. Passed into law by the UK Parliament as the Civic Government

(Scotland) Act 1982.

15. The Civic Government (Scotland) Bill, June 24, 1982.

16. Public Order (Northern Ireland) 1987, SI 1987 463 (NI 7), effective April 2, 1987.

17. R. Sandall and A. R.Wiggins, *The History of The Salvation Army, Vol. II* (London: Salvationist Publishing and Supplies Ltd., 1950), 208.

Chapter 9

1. See Epistle of James.

2. John D. Waldron, ed., *Creed and Deed: Toward a Christian Theology of Social Services in The Salvation Army* (Toronto: The Salvation Army, 1986).

3. Meredith Willson, "With Banner and Bonnets"; 42 U.S.C. 2000.

4. Massachusetts General Law, Chapter 151B.

5. Equal Employment Opportunities Act, 42 U.S.C., section 2000e-1.

6. Ibid.

7. *McLure v. The Salvation Army*, U.S. Court of Appeals for the Fifth Circuit, 460 F2d. 553 (1972).

8. *Corporation of Presiding Bishops v. Amos*, 438 U.S. 325 (1987).

9. Donald E. McNamee, "Status of Employment Practices of Religious Organizations in Massachusetts and Recommendations for The Salvation Army," Legal Opinion, Boston, MA, October 4, 1996.

10. Carvosso Gauntlett, *Social Evils the Army Has Challenged* (London: Salvationist Publishing and Supplies Ltd., 1946).

11. William Booth, *In Darkest England and the Way Out*; Criminal Law Amendment Act 1885

12. Madge Unsworth, *Maiden Tribute* (London: Salvationist Publishing and Supplies Ltd., 1949).

13. *UKWC*, August 15, 1914. Until October 27, 1990 *The War Cry* was published by International Headquarters in London and was known as *The International War Cry*. It was replaced by *Salvationist*, which became a publication of the newly created United Kingdom Territory. *The War Cry* ceased to carry "Official Gazette" announcements after March 15, 1986.

14. Leviticus 18:1–5, *New English Bible*.

Part IV, Prologue

1. *SASB*, 158, Song 573, verse 3.

Chapter 10

1. *The Salvation Army Year Book* (London: The Salvation Army International Headquarters, 1999). Hereafter cited as *SAYB*.

2. Ibid., 38–40.

3. Ibid., 26.

4. Solveig Smith, *By Love Compelled: The Story of The Salvation Army in India and Adjacent Countries* (London: Salvationist Publishing and Supplies Ltd., 1981), chapter 1.

5. Harry Williams, *Booth–Tucker: William Booth's First Gentleman* (London: Hodder and Stoughton, 1980), 165.

6. *SAYB*, 29–30.

7. *SASB*, 230, Song 829, verse 1; 232, Song 833, verse 1; 231, Song 830, verse 1.

8. Shaw Clifton, *Strong Doctrine, Strong Mercy* (London: The Salvation Army, 1985). See chapter 7.

Chapter 11

1. Margaret Burt and Peter Farthing, eds., *Crossing Cultures: How to Manage the Stress of Re–Entry* (Sydney: The Salvation Army, 1996).

2. *Orders and Regulations for Territorial Commanders and Chief Secretaries* (London: The Salvation Army International Headquarters, 1995).

3. Salvation Army Act 1980, c. XXX, Parliament of the United Kingdom, in force on August 1, 1980.

Chapter 12

1. See the author's doctoral dissertation, *The Salvation Army's Actions and Attitudes in Wartime: 1899–1945* (King's College, University of London, 1988) for a detailed study of Salvationist policies and reactions in wartime and of the impact of war upon the work and structures of the Army. Copies are held at the leading Salvation Army archives and heritage centers around the world.

2. Frederick Coutts, *No Continuing City* (London: Hodder and Stoughton, 1976), 150.

3. Catherine Bramwell Booth, *Bramwell Booth* (London: Rich and Cowan, 1933), 353.

4. Frederick Coutts, *Portrait of a Salvationist* (London: Salvationist Publishing and Supplies Ltd., 1955), 18.

5. Sandall and Wiggins, 292. William Booth paid three visits to South Africa: in 1891, 1895 and 1908. See George S. Railton, *General Booth* (London: The Salvation Army, 1912), 147.

6. *UKWC*, October 14, 1899, 1. See also September 30, 1899, 8.

7. *The War Cry* (South Africa: The Salvation Army), June 9, 1900, 1; November 11, 1899; September 30, 1899, 6.

8. *UKWC*, September 30, 1899, 6.

9. William Booth, *The Officer*, November 1899, 402.

10. *UKWC*, October 21, 1899, 8.

11. Ibid., March 31, 1900.

12. Ibid., 8.

13. *All the World* (London: The Salvation Army International Headquarters, March 1900), 190.

14. *UKWC*, June 9, 1900, 8.

15. Ibid., June 7, 1902, 8.

16. E. A. Walker, "The Struggle for Supremacy," *The Cambridge History of the British Empire, Vol. VIII* (Cambridge: Cambridge University Press, 1963), 631.

17. *UKWC*, February 17, 1900, 3. For an account of the Naval and Military League see Frederick Coutts, *The Battle and the Breeze* (London: Salvationist Publishing and Supplies Ltd., 1946).

18. Mary Murray, *The Salvation Army at Work in the Boer War* (London: The Salvation Army International Headquarters, 1901), vii. NML statistics vary according to the source: see T. F. G. Coates, *The Prophet of the Poor: The Life Story of General Booth* (London: Hodder and Stoughton, 1905), 306 where he states that by 1905 there were Leaguers on 100 warships and in over 100 regiments.

19. *UKWC*, August 22, 1914, 9; May 9, 1914, 16 and June 6, 1914, 16; July 4, 1914, 2.

20. Frederick Coutts, *The History of The Salvation Army* (London: Hodder and Stoughton, 1973), 22.

21. Richard Collier, *The General Next to God* (London: Fontana, 1968).

22. *The Officer*, August 1914, 505–508.

23. *UKWC*, October 24, 1914, 6.

24. *All the World*, December 1917, 515.

25. *UKWC*, December 5, 1914, 6; January 2, 1915, 6.

26. *All the World*, May 1915, 230.

27. *The Social Gazette* (London: December 11, 1915), 3; Collier, 226.

28. *UKWC*, October 3, 1914, 8.

29. *The War Cry* (USA: September 12, 1914), 12. Hereafter cited as *USWC*.

30. *SAYB*, 1915, 43; 1916, 52; 1917, 60; 1918, 59–60.

31. Max Gruner, *Revolutionares Christentum* (Berlin: Verlag der Heilsarmee, 1954, Vol. II), 37, 38, 45.

32. *UKWC*, October 3, 1914, 7; October 31, 1914, 7; November 11, 1914, 7; January 16, 1914, 8; January 2, 1915, 8; *All The World*, April 1915, 230.

33. Alexander Damon, Diaries, Salvation Army National Archives, USA, Ref. RG 20.38, entry for December 4, 1917.

34. *USWC*, April 21, 1917, 12.

35. Evangeline Booth and Grace Livingstone Hill, *The War Romance of The Salvation Army* (Toronto: William Briggs, 1919), 49, 147, 151, 192, 214 and 224. Eva wrote the Preface; Hill wrote the text following prolonged

interviews and Eva approved the final text.

36. Helen Purviance, "A Doughgirl on the Firing Line," *The Forum* (New York: December 1918), 648–656.

37. Stella Young, unpublished manuscript at the Salvation Army National Archives, Alexandria, VA. Accession 85-62. See also Evangeline Booth, "Around the World with The Salvation Army," *National Geographic* (April 1920), 347–368. A useful summary of the work of seven War Work organizations, including the Army, is John D. Rockefeller's undated "Service to our Soldiers and Sailors." Greater New York United War Work Campaign committee in Salvation Army National Archives, USA.

38. P. W. Wilson, *General Evangeline Booth of the Salvation Army* (New York: Charles Scribner, 1948), 174.

39. Booth and Hill, 11–24.

40. *USWC*, May 17, 1919, cover; Wilson, 11–24.

41. John Bond, *The Army that Went with the Boys* (Melbourne: The Salvation Army, 1919), vi. This is an explicitly politicized account of war work by Australian Salvationists. See also *The War Cry* (Melbourne: The Salvation Army, October 17, 1914), 8.

42. *The War Cry* (Melbourne: The Salvation Army, December 11, 1915), 11.

43. Catherine Bramwell Booth, 358–359.

44. Ibid.

45. "Report of the Salvation Army's Work in Connection with the Great War 1914–1919" (Salvation Army Archives: Wellington, New Zealand), 57.

46. Ibid., 71.

47. *Britannia Book of the Year, 1946* (Chicago: Encyclopedia Britannica, 1946).

48. E. C. Helmreich, *The German Church Under Hitler* (Detroit: Wayne State University Press, 1979), 384.

49. F. Coutts, *History of The Salvation Army*, 75–76; Sandall and Wiggins, 197; *SAYB*, 1946, 10; *UKWC*, March 22, 1941, 5.

50. Albert Orsborn, *The House of My Pilgrimage* (London: Salvationist Publishing and Supplies Ltd., 1958), 171–172.

51. Alva Holbrook, "One Officer's Experiences in Two World Wars," unpublished manuscript held in Salvation Army National Archives, USA, Accession 85-21.

52. A. W. Brewer, "Report on Attack on Pearl Harbor," unpublished report held in Salvation Army National Archives, USA, Accession 85-27; original deposited in Hawaii War Records Depository, University of Hawaii, Honolulu, September 15, 1944.

53. Paul Johnson, *A History of Christianity* (London: Penguin Books, 1979), 489. Johnson states that one–third of Witnesses were killed, and 97 percent suffered persecution of some sort.

54. F. Coutts, *History of The Salvation Army*, 18.

Epilogue
1. Hebrews 13:8.
2. Isaiah 43:18–19